MW00773131

TEACHING
PSALMS
Volume I

From text to message

CHRISTOPHER ASH

SERIES EDITORS: DAVID JACKMAN & ADRIAN REYNOLDS

TEACHING
PSALMS
Volume I

From text to message

CHRISTOPHER ASH

SERIES EDITORS: DAVID JACKMAN & ADRIAN REYNOLDS

PT RESOURCES

CHRISTIAN
FOCUS

Copyright © Proclamation Trust Media 2017

ISBN: 978-1-52710-004-6

10 9 8 7 6 5 4 3 2 1

Published in 2017, reprinted in 2018
by
Christian Focus Publications Ltd,
Geanies House, Fearn, Ross-shire,
IV20 1TW, Scotland, Great Britain.
www.christianfocus.com

with

Proclamation Trust Resources,
Willcox House, 140-148 Borough High Street,
London, SE1 1LB, England, Great Britain.
www.proctrust.org.uk

Cover design by Moose77.com

Printed and bound by Bell & Bain.

Contents

Author's Preface..9

Series Preface 15

Part One: How to pray the Psalms in Christ 19

   1. We must pray the Psalms 19

   2. We can't pray the Psalms........................31

   3. How to pray the Psalms in Christ 38

   4. Examples of praying the Psalms in Christ ...65

   5. Drawing the lines to Christ 93

Part Two: Difficulties we face in the Psalms 105

   6. Who are 'the righteous' in the Psalms?...... 105

   7. How can we pray Psalms of suffering?...... 114

   8. Can we pray for God's judgment on
       the wicked?...................................... 123

Part Three: Integrating the Psalms into the
Bible story 147

   9. Creation in the Psalms........................... 148

  10. Abraham in the Psalms.......................... 160

  11. Exodus in the Psalms 169

  12. Sinai in the Psalms 180

  13. Zion in the Psalms 189

  14. Exile in the Psalms 197

  15. Lament and Praise in the Psalms............. 205

Part Four: How to teach the Psalms 221

   16. How Hebrew poetry works 221

   17. The fourfold task of the Psalms
       Teacher 231

   18. A Framework for preparing to
       teach a Psalm..................................... 242

   19. Planning a Teaching Series on
       the Psalms 249

Conclusion: How the Psalms reshape our prayers 257

Bibliography 259

   Commentaries on the Psalms........................ 259

   Other Sources 260

To Carolyn, my dear wife and daily prayer-partner

࿐ ࿐ ࿐

Almighty God, you alone can order the unruly wills and passions of sinful men: grant that your people may love what you command and desire what you promise so that among the many and varied changes of this world our hearts may be firmly fixed where true joys are to be found through Jesus Christ our Lord. Amen.[1]

---

1. Collect for fourth Sunday after Easter, taken from *An English Prayer Book* (The Church Society, 1994).

AUTHOR'S PREFACE

I have grown to love the Psalms. It was not always so. At my (very old-fashioned) school we chanted the Psalms and Canticles in daily Chapel services. We didn't chant them well; you wouldn't expect that from 650 schoolboys in the late 1960s and early 1970s. Sometimes we showed what heroic rebels we were by refusing to sing them; but by and large we conformed. Not being sufficiently musical, I did not understand the pointing marks in the chapel Psalter; I didn't know whether the note should go up or down; and I was unsure when it should go wherever it was meant to go. I was completely at sea in understanding the old English of Coverdale's wonderful sixteenth-century translation. It conveyed a kind of atmosphere; I remember that. But no clarity of meaning. I was not yet converted; and even when I was (in my final year in school), I was not edified. The problem was not one of musical incompetence (though I *was* incompetent); it was that nobody taught me to sing the Psalms from the heart with feeling and meaning.

If you love the Psalms, or want to love the Psalms, or think perhaps you ought to love the Psalms (but don't really), these volumes are for you. The proper purpose of singing the Psalms is that we learn to pray them. Psalms have sometimes been sung just for their musical beauty, as a choral performance; but this is not the reason we have them in the Bible. They are here so that we put our hearts into the words as we join in. Whether or not you have a suitable musical accompaniment for singing, and whether you sing them or say them, I hope these volumes will help you pray the Psalms from the heart.

This series of books is for Bible teachers and preachers. Since the Psalms are in the Bible so that we learn to pray them, it follows that the purpose of preaching and teaching the Psalms is to help, equip and motivate us to pray them. So if you have the privilege of preaching, teaching, or leading Bible studies on the Psalms, I hope these books will be of particular help to you. But it is important to remember that a preacher or teacher cannot teach the Psalms until he or she learns to pray them from their own heart. So I want to help you to do that too. It is not as easy as Christians sometimes think. But it is important, and it is possible.

Although I love the Psalms, my love is tinged with frustration at the prevalence of Christless handling of them; or readings to which Christ is a somewhat arbitrary 'add on,' tacked on the end to make it feel 'Christian.' I want first to persuade you that the Psalms are filled with Christ, that Christ does not have to be 'glued on' to the Psalms to make them 'Christian,' but that Christ emerges from the warp and woof of the Psalms themselves. Then I want to equip you to read them Christianly, to pray them in Christ, and to love them in Christ.

I am also frustrated by the near absence of the Psalms from much of our corporate prayer life, and the superficiality and selectivity in the Psalms that we do make reference to. A former student wrote to me that in his experience, 'we do not get any teaching from the Psalms, but only a good feeling, especially when one is downcast.'[1] There is a way of using the Psalms that is like pic'n'mix in a sweet shop; it skims the Psalms for nuggets that appeal, little gems to be printed on the devotional calendar. This has the same nutritional value for our souls that sugary sweets have for our bodies. It is deeply unsatisfactory.

What is more, even when the Psalms *are* taught, it is generally only a small subset of the Psalms. I suspect that an analysis of Psalms sermons would reveal that the large majority come from a mini-psalter within the Psalter, a selection of the favourites. This would include Psalms 1, 2, 8, 23, and so on. But perhaps a hundred or more would scarcely be taught, if at all; and, when they are taught, they are handled selectively; within a chosen Psalm, we pick and choose which verses to teach. J. Clinton McCann comments that, since the Psalms have such an honoured place in Christian history, 'it is all the more strange and striking that the church in relatively recent years has virtually lost the Psalter' and that, even when Psalms are included in metrical versions, 'the selection of Psalms seldom does justice to the rich variety of the Psalter.'[2] I want to broaden my own range, and yours.

Volume One is a handbook to introduce the task, the problems, the method, and some of the main themes. Part One

---

1. from Christopher Thwala, used with permission.
2. McCann 1993b: 13f.

(How to pray the Psalms in Christ) is the core of the argument; it is vital to read and understand this, which is the key to all that follows. Part Four (How to teach the Psalms) gives practical instruction for preachers and Bible teachers. The chapters of Part Two (Difficulties we face in the Psalms) and Part Three (Integrating the Psalms into the Bible story) may be read in any order, and referred to as and when they are helpful.

Volume Two begins with an overview of the structure of the Psalter and then gives a brief Christian introduction to each Psalm; it is not a substitute for a good commentary, but it offers what few commentaries attempt.

The Psalms are an ongoing project for me, both experientially (as I begin to learn to pray) and didactically (as I seek to teach others to pray them). But I feel I have scarcely begun. Luther wrote, 'There is no book of the Bible to which I have devoted as much labour as to the Psalter.'[3] And yet, 'I must openly admit that I do not know whether I have the accurate interpretation of the Psalms or not.'[4] Indeed, he observes with characteristic acuity,

> The Spirit reserves much for Himself, so that we may always remain His pupils. There is much that He reveals only to lure us on, much that He gives only to stir us up...I know that a person would be guilty of the most shameless boldness if he dared claim that he had understood even one book of the Scriptures in all its parts. In fact, who would even dare to assert that anyone has completely understood one single Psalm? Our life is one of beginning and of growth, not one of consummation.[5]

---

3. Quoted in Brock 2007:169.

4. Brock 2007:169.

5. Brock 2007:169.

If that was true of Luther, it is certainly true of me! But I hope, in the mercy of God, that even these introductory volumes may be of help.

This handbook began life as a short course on how to teach and preach Bible poetry, given year by year at The Proclamation Trust Cornhill Training Course from 2004. After a while this developed into a full-blown course on the Psalms, which continued at Cornhill until June 2016. The enthusiasm, hunger, encouragement, and searching questions of the five hundred or so students on the course over those years have been my main stimulus for writing. I have also been helped and encouraged by conversations and practical help from former colleagues at the Proclamation Trust, and especially from Adrian and Celia Reynolds.

I am also grateful for many opportunities to preach and teach Psalms, in particular at the Evangelical Ministry Assembly in London, at the 'Basics' Conference at Parkside Church, Ohio, at Morling College in Sydney, and at Queensland Theological College in Brisbane. The facilities and the fellowship generously given by Tyndale House in Cambridge have been invaluable.

SERIES PREFACE

We now understand that those called to preach and teach the word of God need to have a firm grasp of biblical theology: the way the whole Bible story unfolds and fits together culminating in the coming, death, resurrection, ascension and return of Jesus Christ. Our *Teaching* series, with its aim of equipping and encouraging those called to this great task, lets the discipline of biblical theology (alongside its co-disciplines) sit firmly at the centre of our work.

It is quite disappointing therefore that so little effort has been made to apply this important methodology to the Psalms. We've worked hard at New Testament narrative, epistles, Old Testament story and even Law, but given very little time to the 150 Hebrew poems that make up what we sometimes call the Psalter. This omission is even more surprising because we often sing or pray the psalms in church and give psalms to new or inexperienced preachers, sometimes as summer 'fillers' in a quieter preaching season.

These two volumes then are some of the most important we have published. Whilst some of our other sixteen volumes in the series are those a preacher might dip into when needing some help with a particular Bible passage, these contributions from Christopher need to be read more carefully. That means that we have taken a slightly different approach from other volumes in the series. There is an argument to be made before we get to the detailed work on a psalm by psalm basis. Volume 1 is the basis for this argument and needs to be read carefully. Volume 2 builds on this argument (and largely assumes it) as Christopher takes us through the psalms one by one.

Readers should not suppose that this way of approaching the psalter is novel or radical. As others have shown, the desire to understand the psalms in their whole Bible Christological context is as old as Christianity itself.[1] All through Christian history, preachers have returned again to the struggle to be faithful to the biblical theology of the psalms. Writing in the nineteenth century, this understanding was neatly summarised by Free Church of Scotland minister Andrew Bonar, 'The writers were prepared by God, through personal and public circumstances, for breathing forth appropriately the mind of Him [Christ] who used them.'[2]

Despite the fact that these books may feel a little different from others we have previously published in this series, our ultimate aim for them remains the same: we trust and pray that men and women who are called to preach and teach the word of God will be encouraged and

---

1. See, for example, Jerry Shepherd's doctoral thesis submitted to Westminster Theological Seminary in 1995, available online at http://bit.ly/2figu43.

2. Bonar, Andrew, *Christ and his church in the Book of Psalms* (London, James Nisbet & Co, 1859), p. vi.

equipped to do so faithfully and clearly in a way that exalts the Saviour above all.

Our thanks go to Celia Reynolds for proof reading and her checking of cross references, Crystal Williams for correcting and updating manuscripts and – especially – to our friends at Christian Focus for their gospel partnership in this important project.

DAVID JACKMAN &
ADRIAN REYNOLDS
Series Editors
London 2016

Part One:

HOW TO PRAY THE PSALMS IN CHRIST

Part One outlines the central argument and method of this handbook. Here is a way of reading the Psalms in Christ that has a long Christian history, but will involve a paradigm shift for some readers. I want to persuade you that this does justice to the original meaning of the Psalms and their place in the whole Bible story. Further, I want to whet your appetite that this way of praying the Psalms is not only true but also fruitful in shaping our prayers and praises.

1. We must pray the psalms

You and I need to pray. Those who 'call on the name of the Lord' will be saved (Joel 2:32), and that is what prayer is.[1] Prayer is our life-blood; if we pray, we live to God; if we do not pray, we do not. Not simply at the start of the Christian life, but every day until we die or Jesus returns. Prayer is an urgent and ever-present necessity.

---

1. Millar 2016.

We need to be taught to pray

What is more, we need to be taught to pray. When God drew me to faith in Christ as a teenager at a summer camp, we used to have a Bible talk on prayer every year. One of the regular ingredients of those talks ran something like this: 'It is a wonderful thing to belong to Jesus. Jesus has brought you to God the Father by His death on the cross and now you can pray to God as your Father and know that He hears you. You don't need to use set prayers or prayers written by others; it doesn't need to be formal; you can just talk to God, and that is what prayer is. Through Jesus Christ we have access to the Father by the Spirit (see Eph. 2:18).'

That is a glorious truth and, as a very young Christian, it warmed my heart. But it is not the whole truth. For you and I do need to be taught to pray. Prayer is more than just saying whatever you want to God. John tells us that 'if we ask anything according to [God's] will, he hears us' (1 John 5:14). But how do we know what is according to God's will? Jesus promises that when we pray in His name, prayer will be heard and answered (John 14:14, 16:23,26). But what does it mean to pray in Jesus' name?

The Psalms teach us to pray

John the Baptist taught his disciples how to pray; Jesus' disciples asked, 'Lord, teach us to pray, just as John taught his disciples' (Luke 11:1). Jesus answered with the pattern we call the Lord's Prayer (Luke 11:2-4 and Matt. 6:9-13). But the Lord's Prayer is the tip of a great Bible iceberg of God teaching and training us to pray, of which the Psalms are perhaps the most significant part. They were the corporate prayers of the Old Covenant people of God. So, for example, 2 Samuel 22:1-51 is David's song or prayer; and it became Psalm 18, Israel's song or prayer. Luther wrote that the Psalter 'is interwoven with the Our Father [the Lord's Prayer] in such a way that we can understand each through the other very well and see their happy harmony.'

The New Covenant people of God continued to use the Psalms. A Spirit-filled church will speak 'to one another with psalms, hymns and songs from the Spirit' (Eph. 5:19); we are probably not to understand these as three different categories, so that something is either a Psalm or a hymn or a song from the Spirit (with the last of these being the most spiritual!). Rather, these words are three ways of speaking of spiritual (Spirit-given) songs. (The adjective translated 'from the Spirit' 'refers to all three nouns.'[2]) The three words, 'psalms', 'hymns' and 'songs', 'are the most common words used in the Greek Old Testament[3] for religious songs, and occur interchangeably in the titles of the Psalms.'[4] So, just as the designation 'psalm' can (obviously) refer to an Old Testament Psalm, so the designations 'hymn' and 'song' can also refer to an Old Testament Psalm. Paul says something very similar in Colossians 3:16. It is clear from these verses that, while we cannot conclude that the early church used *only* Old Testament Psalms, these formed a significant, and perhaps the main, part of their Spirit-inspired singing. In his excellent biblical theology of prayer, Gary Millar writes, 'the psalter as a whole provides us with the most detailed and sustained treatment of how God's people can, should and must call on him.'[5]

---

2. O'Brien 1999:365.

3. The Septuagint (LXX).

4. O'Brien 1999:395.

5. Millar 2016:140.

Mainstream Christian history has followed in this tradition. In 'the first few centuries of the Christian era' the Psalms generated 'far more commentaries than any other biblical book. More importantly, by at least the fourth century, the book of Psalms was being used as a *Psalter*, a songbook that was in constant – often daily – liturgical and private use.'[6] One historian comments that, 'By the fourth century the memorisation of the Psalms by many Christians and their habitual use as songs in worship by all Christians...were matters of long-standing tradition.'[7] Later, the monastic communities of the middle ages recited the Psalms as a regular part of their liturgy. In the Rule of St Benedict (c. 530) all 150 Psalms were to be completed each week.[8]

When set Bible readings began to be adopted in services (a Lectionary), the singing of a Psalm was not regarded as a reading so much as a response to the other scriptures read.[9] This raises a significant question: in what way are we to understand the Psalms (and other prayers and songs of Scripture) to be 'the word of God'? It is easy to understand how the voices of the law, the prophets, the gospels, and the epistles are the word of God, for in them God speaks 'down' (as it were) to us through the mouth of His prophets, His Son, and His apostles; they are what God speaks to us. But what of the parts of Scripture which are spoken 'up' from men and women to God? In one sense they are the responses of believers to the word that God has spoken 'down' to them;

6. Brock 2007:xii.

7. Holladay 1996:165.

8. Holladay 1996:177.

9. Holladay 1996:177.

and yet they are more than that. Athanasius wrote that the Psalms 'have a unique place in the Bible because most of the Scripture speaks to us, while the Psalms speak *for* us.'[10] They are not the same as other prayers prayed by believers down the generations; they are Bible prayers. They are not just response; they are authorised response, the words God gives us with which to speak 'up' to Him. They are 'the word *from* God to be spoken *to* God'. In other words, they teach us to pray.

In Luther's *Preface to the Psalter* he wrote, 'As a teacher will compose letters or little speeches for his pupils to write to their parents, so by this book He prepares both the language and the mood in which we should address the Heavenly Father.'[11]

So the Psalms teach us to pray. Here are six related blessings that come from praying the Psalms.

The Psalms train us to respond to the riches of Bible truth

Early in the fourth century, Athanasius wrote a wonderful letter to Marcellinus, a friend who had been ill and used his illness 'to study the whole body of the Holy Scriptures and especially the Psalms' (what a wonderful way to use an illness!). Athanasius writes to help him with the Psalms.

---

10. Anderson 1970:x.

11. quoted in Brock 2007:171 or this from Calvin, 'Now what Saint Augustine says is true, that no one is able to sing things worthy of God unless he has received them from him. Wherefore, when we have looked thoroughly everywhere and searched high and low, we shall find no better songs nor more appropriate for the purpose than the Psalms of David, which the Holy Spirit made and spoke through him. And furthermore, when we sing them, we are certain that God puts the words in our mouths, as if he himself were singing in us to exalt his glory'. Epistle to the Reader from the *1542 Geneva Psalter*, quoted by Holladay 1996:200.

He describes each book of the Bible as 'like a garden which grows one special kind of fruit' and then says that, 'by contrast, the Psalter is a garden which, besides its special fruit, grows also those of all the rest.'

Luther wrote that the Psalter, 'might well be called a little Bible. In it is comprehended most beautifully and briefly everything that is in the entire Bible.'[12] One scholar comments that, 'of all the books of the Bible, of the Old Testament at any rate, the Psalter was closest to (Luther's) heart...On no other part of the Bible did he lavish so much time, energy and sheer love.'[13] Calvin says that in the Psalms, 'there is nothing wanting which relates to the knowledge of eternal salvation.'[14]

In the fourth century, Ambrose wrote that, 'Although all Scripture breathes the grace of God, yet sweet beyond all others is the Book of the Psalms. *History* instructs, the *Law* teaches, *Prophecy* announces, rebukes, chastens, *Morality* persuades; but in the Book of Psalms we have the fruit of these, and a kind of medicine for the salvation of men.'[15]

On the frontispiece of his wonderful early twentieth-century commentary, A. F. Kirkpatrick prints this from Richard Hooker; I have translated into modern English to make it more understandable:

> The Psalms contain in brief the very best and most beautiful things from all the books of the Bible, and express these

---

12. Luther 1960:254.

13. Heinz Bluhm, quoted in Brock 2007:168.

14. *Preface to Commentary on the Psalms*, Calvin Vol. IV p. xxxix.

15. Quoted by Herbert Lockyer, 'In Wonder of the Psalms,' *Christianity Today* 28.4, March 2, 1984, p. 76. I am grateful to John F. Evans for drawing my attention to this quotation.

in a way that moves us, because of their poetry...What do people need to know which the Psalms are not able to teach us? For beginners they give easy instruction, for all of us a mighty strengthening of virtue and knowledge, and strong assurance. Heroic generosity, exquisite justice, serious thought, precise wisdom, genuine repentance, untiring patience, the wonders of God, the sufferings of Christ, the terrors of God's wrath, the comforts of God's grace, God's providence all over the world, and the promised joys of the world to come, are all to be found here. You cannot find a grief or sickness we experience, for which there is not a remedy in this treasure-house, ready to be found at all times.[16]

So, when learning to teach and to pray the Psalms, we have a rich treat in store.

The Psalms shape well-rounded human beings to pray in all of human life

The Psalms express every facet of human experience and arise from every circumstance of human life. A student commented to me that the Psalms are causing him to have a richer and broader palette of emotional colours with which to describe his own, and others', experience. 'It is my view,' wrote the church father Athanasius, 'that in the words of this book [the Psalter] the whole human life, its basic spiritual conduct and as well its occasional movements and thoughts, is comprehended and contained. Nothing to be found in human life is omitted.'[17] John Calvin calls the Psalms, 'An Anatomy of all the Parts of the Soul' because 'there is not an emotion of which any one can be conscious that is not here

---

16. Kirkpatrick 1892-1903:viii (I am grateful to John Evans for drawing my attention to this quotation).

17. Athanasius, *Letter to Marcellinus*.

represented as in a mirror. Or, rather, the Holy Spirit has here drawn to the life all the griefs, sorrows, fears, doubts, hopes, cares, perplexities, in short, all the distracting emotions with which the minds of men are wont to be agitated.'[18]

The Psalms reshape disordered human affections into God's good order

The task of a minister of the gospel is deeper than reforming the actions and words of the men and women entrusted to our care; it is to see changed hearts. Only God can change the human heart; but He does it through the ministry of the gospel word with prayer. The Psalms have a significant role to play in this work.

The Psalms are necessary because we are totally depraved. This does not mean that we are as evil as we could possibly be; that would make us into demons, and would deny the truths of God's common grace, whereby human beings are capable, for example, of acts of love and self-sacrifice. What it does mean is that no facet of our human personhood is immune from the tainting disease of sin. When our family moved into a rather ugly house, my wife bought a couple of wooden flower tubs to improve the appearance of the front entrance. I was tasked with boring drainage holes, so I took my bit and brace and drilled away. As I did so, there was an unmistakeable whiff of whisky. Every grain of that wood had been soaked in whisky during the years it had served as a whisky barrel. I could have drilled anywhere and found the same. In the same way, every facet of human personhood is tainted by sin. Our thinking is twisted, so that we cannot think as we ought to think. Our wills are distorted, so that we do not decide as we ought to decide. Our bodies

---

18. Calvin, *Preface*:xxxvii.

are spoiled, so that natural appetites grow out of proper proportion, or enslave us in the grip of addictive behaviours.

What is more – and this is where the Psalms especially come in – our affections, desires and aversions are disordered. We are attracted by what we ought not to desire, and we are untouched by what ought to delight us. We desire and delight in what we ought to shrink from and hate; and we care little for what we ought deeply to desire. For example, we long for the praise of others while struggling to rejoice when others succeed. We are inwardly sad when others rejoice at some promotion or some success in love, wishing their success had been ours; and we may even secretly be just a little pleased when they fail, in the ugly feeling we call *schadenfreude*. Far from rejoicing with those who rejoice and weeping with those who weep, sometimes we weep inwardly at the joy of others and are gleeful at the weeping of our rivals. We love our pleasures and comfort while caring little for the honour of God and the glory of Jesus.

The Psalms not only train us to pray; they gradually reshape our affections and our aversions so that we love what we ought to love and hate what we ought to hate.

The Church of England Collect for the fourth Sunday after Easter expresses it beautifully like this:

> O Almighty God, who alone canst order the unruly wills and affections of sinful men: Grant unto thy people, that they may love the thing which thou commandest, and desire that which thou dost promise; that so, among the sundry and manifold changes of the world, our hearts may surely there be fixed, where true joys are to be found; through Jesus Christ our Lord. Amen.[19]

_____

19. *Book of Common Prayer*, Collect for Fourth Sunday after Easter.

I have an unruly will, which desires all manner of goals, some fairly good, some downright evil, most ambiguous. I have disordered affections, that sweep me this way and that like wild waves on a stormy sea. I need Almighty God to order these. I know what He commands, and I know that I ought to do what He commands. But I need Almighty God to work in me so that I *love* what He commands, so that I deeply love humility, purity, justice, honesty, generosity, and so on. I know from the Bible what He promises me in Christ; I need Almighty God so to work in me that my great desire in life is to inherit those promises, rather than to gain some of 'the kingdoms of the world and their glory' (Matt. 4:8 ESV). In all this, the Psalms will shape my affections and aversions into godly paths.

The German Lutheran pastor and scholar Dietrich Bonhoeffer understood the Psalms as a 'children's primer' to teach us how to talk to God, and to train our speech and our affections towards God.[20]

When the charismatic movement swept across British and North American Christianity in the 1960s, one of the sad consequences was the loss of proper emotion in some conservative churches. In reaction against errors within the charismatic movement, in which emotion became disordered emotionalism, those who defined themselves as conservative or classical evangelicals sometimes retreated into a spiritual life with very little emotion. This was a strange historical anomaly for those whose forefathers had been nicknamed 'enthusiasts,'[21] and it meant that a young Christian in a conservative church might look across the

---

20. quoted in Brock 2007:74.

21. Knox 1950.

street at the emotion of a charismatic church and wonder, by contrast, if his or her own church did emotion at all! The Psalms show us how to develop strong and godly affections, and indeed fierce and healthy aversions as well. They train us to avoid both the unpredictable reefs of charismatic error and the deserts of a dusty orthodoxy. For the Psalms perfectly combine thought and feeling, theology and prayer, emotion and reality, the subjective and the objective.

The Psalms can sweeten sour emotions

I remember visiting a mangrove swamp in a tidal river estuary on an Indonesian island off the coast of Singapore. As I understand it, the reason mangroves can grow in salt water is that they have within themselves some biological mechanism (a filter system in their roots) that turns deadly salt water into life-giving fresh water inside the plant.

The Psalms have a similar ability to take death-giving emotions and turn them into life-giving feelings. In the Preface to his commentary on the Psalms, Calvin writes that the Psalms not only portray emotions, but they show us how to express them. In particular, 'they will principally teach and train us to bear the cross...so that the afflictions which are the bitterest and most severe to our nature, become sweet to us, because they proceed from him.'[22]

In so doing, the Psalms do not manipulate our feelings, as a mood-inducing drug might do; they do not give us a 'high'. What they do is to change our feelings by helping us to grasp the facts. They take the word of God spoken 'down' to us and enable us to respond in a way that is in line with these truths.

---

22. Calvin, *Preface*:xxxix.

The Psalms are a corrective against
idiosyncratic or individualistic piety

Another blessing is that the Psalms express a healthy corporate solidarity with the people of Christ all over the world and in every age.

One scholar writes this:

> whenever you read the Psalms, when you sing them or pray them, you are praying, singing, and reading alongside a huge crowd of faithful witnesses throughout the ages. The words you speak have been spoken thousands – even millions – of times before…. As you read or sing or pray, off to your right stand Moses and Miriam, in front of you David and Solomon kneel down,…while from behind come the voices of Jerome, St Augustine,…Luther, Calvin, and more – so many more![23]

This corporate dimension enables us to relate to God, not as isolated individualists, but as members of a great multi-generational, multi-ethnic, multi-cultural, multi-national people whose history goes on for century after century. The Psalms are a God-given safeguard against isolation in prayer and idiosyncratic ways of relating to God ('I like to relate to God like this…'). They tie us to the long history of the people of God before and after Christ. Always in the Psalms our response is on the journey from 'I' to 'we'.

The Psalms arouse us to warmth in
our relationship with God

By nature we are cold towards God. Another blessing of the Psalms is to warm our cold hearts. In 1537 Calvin drew up the articles for the conduct of worship in Geneva. In them he wrote:

---

23. Wilson 2002:14.

> Furthermore it is a thing most expedient for the edification of the church to sing some Psalms in the form of public prayers by which one prays to God or sings His praises so that the hearts of all may be aroused and stimulated to make similar prayers and to render similar praises and thanks to God with a common love.
>
> Certainly at present the prayers of the faithful are so cold that we should be greatly ashamed and confused. The Psalms can stimulate us to raise our hearts to God and arouse us to an ardour in invoking as well as in exalting with praises the glory of His name.[24]

As we join in the Psalms, our hearts begin to feel and to respond as they did. We conclude that we need to pray, we need to be taught to pray, and we need to learn to pray the Psalms – all the Psalms in their rich entirety. The benefits will be deep and lasting. And yet it is not so easy as we think or hope. We shall face honestly in the next chapter the overwhelming difficulties we face when we embark on this wonderful and yet daunting project.

2. We can't pray the Psalms

The Psalms teach us to pray. Many love them. When we want a slimmed down Bible to fit in a pocket, publishers offer us 'The New Testament and Psalms.' When ministers plan a summer holiday preaching series with occasional preachers, they sometimes say to them, 'Pick your favourite Psalm and preach that.' But when we look closely at the Psalms, we find that what we really love is not the Psalms as a whole, but our favourite nuggets from the Psalms.

By 'praying the Psalms' we do not mean 'praying *from* the Psalms.' The latter invites us to pick and choose which bits of

---

24. Holladay 1996:199.

the Psalms we use as a resource for prayer. We may call this the 'calendar verse' approach; we read a Psalm and see if any of it resonates with our experience and warms our hearts. If it does, we choose that verse to put on one of those old-fashioned devotional calendars. January: 'The Lord is my shepherd, I lack nothing.' February: 'Taste and see that the Lord is good; blessed is the one who takes refuge in him.' And so on.

This may make us feel better but, if this is all we do, it lacks integrity. For if God has given us the Psalms to teach us to pray, then we must learn to pray the Psalms God has given us, and not just the parts that we like. For if we pick and choose, we might as well learn to pray by finding blessed thoughts from the Archers or East Enders. For it is we who are in charge, choosing what we like.

But the moment we resolve to pray the Psalms as a whole, missing nothing, changing nothing, we come face to face with a mountain of problems. It is a useful exercise to go through a Psalm line by line making a note of which parts do not fit – and cannot reasonably be made to fit – your individual experience. This will yield plenty of problems, even when you make a reasonable allowance for reading poetic expressions metaphorically.

When teaching the Psalms, I have sometimes set students an exercise. I have printed side by side the text of Psalm 23 and the lyrics of Stuart Townend's deservedly popular metrical version ('The Lord's my shepherd, I'll not want' with its chorus 'And I will trust in you alone'). I have then asked the students which parts of the Psalm have been omitted in the song, and to consider why they think this might be. Making due allowance for the kinds of changes necessary to put the Psalm into a metrical form, this exercise yields two main answers.

First, the song omits reference to 'for his name's sake' in verse 3 of the Psalm. David says of the Lord that, 'He leads me in paths of righteousness *for his name's sake*.' That is to say, 'God leads me to live rightly because his reputation depends upon it. If I go astray, people will think worse of God; his name will suffer. He needs to keep me on the right path for the sake of his reputation.' We see something similar in Psalm 25:11 ('For the sake of your name, Lord, forgive my iniquity...') and Psalm 31:3 ('for the sake of your name lead and guide me'). We can understand why this might be omitted. After all, you and I feel a little arrogant making such a claim. We may sing that God in His kindness keeps us on the right path. But it is hard to see how His reputation depends upon it. Why should *His* reputation be tied to *my* morality?

Second, the song does not include any version of verse 5a, in which David says, 'You prepare a table before me in the presence of my enemies.' That is to say, 'You sit me down at a victory feast, while my defeated enemies can only look on in despair.' Again, it is not difficult to see why this might be felt inappropriate in the song. After all, it seems to make a boast that is too big for my little boots.

In addition, students often note that the song does include one slightly awkward reference, when we are invited to sing, 'And he anoints my head with oil.' Even supposing this to be metaphorical, as we will need to do, it is not immediately clear what it might mean.

None of this is to criticise a deservedly popular and lovely song! It is simply to note that even this old favourite of the Psalms contains elements that do not easily fit into our immediate experience.

Some of these elements may be prayed by using biblical theology to translate them from an Old Covenant to a New

Covenant context; for example, from Zion through Jesus to the local church. We shall consider how to do this in Part Three. But some are more intractable than that. The apparently insoluble difficulties may broadly be considered under five headings.

The Experience of Intense Suffering

There are times when the Psalmists seem to be experiencing suffering so intense that it is difficult for me to identify with it, even on my bad days. Take, for example, some verses from Psalm 88.

> I am overwhelmed with troubles and my life draws near to death…I am set apart with the dead, like the slain who lie in the grave…You have taken from me my closest friends and have made me repulsive to them. I am confined and cannot escape…From my youth I have suffered and been close to death; I have borne your terrors and am in despair… (from vv. 3, 5, 8, 15).

Although this is one of the darker Psalms, the language is not unique. And it is very strong. Even at my gloomiest, I struggle honestly to echo it all. Of course, there are times – perhaps of serious illness or bereavement – when this may resonate. Nonetheless, there is an intensity here that suggests the Psalm is perhaps not intended for me personally. I can sometimes approximate this experience, but I can never plumb its depths. And therefore I have a problem of integrity in trying to make these prayers my own.

Implications of global significance

Again and again, David implies that his being victorious is necessary for the sake of the world. Here is an example from Psalm 118. 'All the nations surrounded me, but in the name of the Lord I cut them down. They surrounded me on every side, but in the name of the Lord I cut them down' (vv. 10-11). It is hard to see how this can be my direct experience, even if I have experienced some problems in my workplace and have overcome them! No, these are the words of one who commands armies and is engaged in international warfare. This is much bigger than me.

Claims to extraordinary innocence

It is sometimes hard to take seriously the seemingly exaggerated claims to innocence or piety made by the Psalmists. Here is an example from Psalm 17. David claims,

> Though you probe my heart, though you examine me at night and test me, you will find that I have planned no evil...My steps have held to your paths; my feet have not stumbled (vv. 3, 5).

This is very searching language. David says that if God had a moral scanner that detected, not just his actions and words, but every movement, every desire, every hope, every affection, of his heart, then at no point would God detect anything amiss. This is extraordinary! I can certainly not claim this; or, if I do, I should rightly be accused of pharisaical hypocrisy. Just what did David mean by it? We want to ask him if he said this before Bathsheba (in which case he was being at best naïve about his heart) or after Bathsheba (which would make it appear a downright lie).

How do we react when we are asked to say, 'I will praise the Lord all my life; I will sing praise to my God as long as I live' (Ps. 146:2)? I suppose we can say it with our fingers crossed behind our backs and actually mean something like, 'I (hope I) will praise the Lord all (or at least most of) my life; I (might) sing praise to my God as long as (or a bit more of the time that) I live.' Or we can say it with naïve optimism.

Or we can be honest and say that it expresses something that is just too strong for our fragile piety.

And then, again and again, the Psalmists cry to God for vindication. They claim to be in the right and call on God to do the right thing by rescuing them. I struggle to feel I can do this, because I am aware of my own sinful heart. I am very aware that it is not justice I need, but mercy and forgiveness. So here is another difficulty with praying all the Psalms.

Praying for God's judgment on the wicked
We feel especially awkward when the words of a Psalm invite us to pray that God will destroy the wicked, not least because we would be praying for our own destruction. And yet the Psalmists do this frequently, and not just in the Psalms usually classified as Imprecatory. So, to take one example, we love Psalm 139 with its well-known and loved affirmations that 'you created my inmost being; you knit me together in my mother's womb....I am fearfully and wonderfully made...' and so on. And yet, just as we are revelling in the precious truths of a lovely Psalm (and thinking some of them would go well on our devotional calendar), we hit verses 19-22 and find ourselves being asked to pray, 'If only you, God, would slay the wicked!... Do I not hate those who hate you, Lord...?' How are we meant to pray this? So here is a fourth difficulty with praying the Psalms.

The strange mixture of singulars and plurals
The last problem is of a rather different kind. In a number of Psalms there is a strange movement between a singular singer ('I') and plural singers ('we' or 'they'). Take, for example, Psalm 145, in which there are several singular/plural movements.

Here is one: 'They speak of the glorious splendour of your majesty – and I will meditate on your wonderful works' (v. 5). We wonder who 'they' are and who is the singular 'I'.

Conclusion

My students once produced for me a collection of inappropriate Psalms verses on something we might have called 'Not the Devotional Calendar.' On the front cover they printed, 'For my life is spent with sorrow and my years with sighing' (Ps. 31:10 ESV). For August we had, 'You have sold your people for a trifle, demanding no high price for them' (Ps. 44:12 ESV), for November 'Moab is my washbasin' (Ps. 60:8). And so on. It was light-hearted mischief. But it reinforced the point that our devotional favourites are just that, the favourites we have chosen. But if we have to pray every verse of all the Psalms, we find ourselves in many and varied difficulties.

All these difficulties make praying the Psalms apparently impossible. We are between a rock and a hard place. On the one hand, we are to acknowledge that the Psalms are authorised response to God. So, for example, Athanasius, in his *Letter to Marcellinus*, writes,

> No one must allow himself to be persuaded, by any arguments whatever, to decorate the Psalms with extraneous matter or make alterations in their order or change the words themselves. They must be sung and chanted in entire simplicity, just as they are written, so that…the Spirit, Who spoke by the saints, recognizing the selfsame words that He inspired, may join us in them too. [25]

If we are to pray Holy Spirit words, we must pray the Psalms undiluted, unmodified, in their entirety.

---

25. www.athanasius.com/psalms/aletterm.htm – accessed 25th October 2016.

But, on the other hand, we cannot honestly do this. So what are we to do? If we abandon the Psalms, and just sing songs or hymns, we deny the God-given way of learning to pray; but if we sing the Psalms as our own individual songs, we have to have our fingers crossed behind our backs when we cannot really mean what they sing.

We need to face these difficulties head on, which we shall now do in chapters three and four. I want to put into your hands a pair of spectacles that you can use to bring the Psalms into focus and make them songs you can pray with integrity as a Christian man or woman today.

3. How to pray the Psalms in Christ

The Old Testament scriptures 'are able to make you wise for salvation through faith in Jesus Christ' (2 Tim. 3:15). But how do the Psalms in particular do this? We come now to what Dietrich Bonhoeffer calls 'the secret of the Psalter.'[26] This is not a mystical secret, brought out like a rabbit from a magician's hat. This is the secret to which the original context of the Psalms points and to which the New Testament adds its clear signposts. There is one way – and one way only – in which the Psalms can become our prayers and praises.

Five considerations lead us to understand the Psalms as the songs supremely of Jesus, that Jesus is the great singer of the Psalms; it is His voice we hear praying, lamenting, teaching, and praising. The Psalms are Christian scripture.[27]

---

26. Bonhoeffer 2005:54.

27. See also Millar 2016:140-154. In answer to the question, 'Whose prayers are these?' Millar concludes, 'a persuasive case can be made for the fact that many of these prayers should be considered "prayers of the Messiah", as he calls on Yahweh to act on his promises.' (p. 154).

We pray the Psalms in Christ because of the role of David the Anointed King

We begin working towards the solution by going right back to the original contexts of the Psalms. Let us leave to one side the question of how we may learn to make them our own prayers. Instead, let us ask what it meant for the original writers and for Old Covenant singers. It is important never to leave behind the original contexts of the Psalms. Often we don't know much about the details of the authors or the circumstances in which the Psalms were written and prayed. But they were all composed and expressed by members of the people of God in the Old Covenant era. Decontextualising the Psalms lacks integrity and risks imposing on them an arbitrary meaning.[28]

However, the point I want us to notice is this: within the original meaning and contexts of the Psalms themselves, there is an unresolved tension that points us forward towards Christ.

In this chapter I am going to put forward an old but neglected model for reading the Psalms Christianly. It is important for us to understand that this model is not being imposed on the Psalms *in spite of* their actual meaning, but arises from the Psalms *because of* their original meaning. To read the Psalms in a way that centres on Christ is to read them according to their original meaning.

We first meet this tension when we enter by the front door of the Psalter through Psalms 1 and 2. Three markers indicate that these two Psalms function as the Introduction to the Psalter. First, by contrast with almost all the Psalms

---

28. 'If we read and use them so as to dissolve them completely into our sensibilities and consciousness, they become merely empty vessels of language that we fill with our own meanings'. Mays 1994:8.

in Book 1, they have no superscription. Almost all the rest are headed 'A Psalm of David'. Second, each ends with a way that leads to destruction. So 'the way of the wicked leads to destruction' (Ps. 1:6); and if you do not 'kiss the Son' to show your allegiance, 'your way will lead to your destruction' (Ps. 2:12). Third, these Psalms are bracketed by declarations of the man who is blessed. Psalm 1 begins with this: 'Blessed is the one who...' (v. 1). Psalm 2 ends with it: 'Blessed are all who take refuge in him' (v. 12).

These introductory Psalms establish two foundational themes right at the outset of the Psalter: God's law and God's king. Psalm 1 declares a blessing on the one who delights in the law of the Lord and destruction for the one who does not. As we read through the Psalms, neither of these declarations appears to be true. Those who delight in the law of the Lord experience many sufferings (e.g. 'The arrogant dig pits to trap me, contrary to your law.... Help me, for I am being persecuted without cause' Ps. 119:85-86) while those who care nothing for the law of the Lord prosper (e.g. '...when I saw the prosperity of the wicked' Ps. 73:3). Each of these observations would seem to contradict Psalm 1. And yet, right near the end of the Psalter, Psalm 145 reaffirms, '[The Lord] fulfils the desires of those who fear him; he hears their cry and saves them. The Lord watches over all who love him, but all the wicked he will destroy' (Ps. 145:19-20). So the Psalter believes this from beginning to end, in spite of the evidence to the contrary.

Then, in Psalm 2, the Lord decrees that the King will be His Son and rule the world. And yet, by the end of the Psalter, there is no king at all in David's line (e.g. 'You have renounced the covenant with your servant – the Davidic king – and have defiled his crown in the dust' Ps. 89:39), let alone one who rules the world. So Psalm 2 does not seem to be true either. And yet Psalm 2 remains in the Psalter, and is reaffirmed in Psalm 110, in Book 5; indeed the covenant with David is reaffirmed in Psalm 132; believers still sang it, despite the evidence.

The tension continues in the Psalms that arise from the life of King David himself, mainly in Books 1 and 2, but also later in the Psalter. For this king knows what it is to suffer greatly, to be rejected, to cry out for vindication, and yet to have the confidence that the Lord will be his deliverer and will crown him with honour in the end. In the life of David, there were two periods in particular that are significant. First, the long period between his anointing by the prophet Samuel and his finally coming into the kingdom (1 Sam. 16–31), first in Judah and then the united kingdom of Judah and Israel (2 Sam. 2:4, 7 and 2 Sam. 5:3). During these years David is the anointed but unrecognised King. Second, there are the terrible days of Absalom's rebellion (2 Sam. 13–19), when his kingship was threatened by a usurper. These two periods especially give rise to many Psalms in which the unrecognised or challenged king cries to God for victory and vindication, so that the promise of Psalm 2 can be fulfilled. And yet, as Old Testament history continues, it never is.

We see the same tension at the start and end of the books of Samuel. In 1 Samuel 2:1-10, in one of the very first Psalms, Hannah rejoices that God will 'give strength to his king and exalt the horn (strength) of his anointed,' despite that fact that at this stage there is no king. She prays by the Spirit, who indicates to her that there will be a king. As 1 Samuel unfolds, that king appears, in chapter 16 when David is anointed by her son Samuel. And then, right near the end of 1 and 2 Samuel, we read David's last words in 2 Samuel 23:1-7. These words tie closely to Psalms 1 and 2, reaffirming the covenant of 2 Samuel 7, but tying it to the King who rules 'in righteousness,' that is to say, the King who fulfils Psalm 1. James Mays says of these words that,

> The idea that David's words might be the word of the Lord about the future messianic king and kingdom begins with this final poem in the narrative of Samuel.

Roland de Vaux comments that,

> In fact, none of [the historical kings] fulfilled this ideal (of Pss. 1 and 2 together), but at the moment of enthronement, at each renewal of the Davidic covenant, the same hope was expressed, in the belief that one day it would be fulfilled. All these texts, then, are Messianic, for they contain a prophecy and a hope of salvation, which an individual chosen by God will bring to fulfilment.[29]

When we take seriously the fact that so many of the Psalms are written by David the king, a number of our difficulties begin to come into focus. First, there is the experience of intense suffering, when hiding from the persecution by King Saul and when fleeing the rebellion of Absalom. These sufferings of King David become 'typical' of the sufferings of later Israel as a whole and anticipate the sufferings of the Messiah as the unrecognised King waiting to come into His kingdom (rather as Tolkien so vividly echoed the theme with Aragorn in *The Lord of the Rings*). After the end of the Davidic monarchy, ended by the Babylonians in 589 B.C., believers in Israel looked back to 'the king, pursued and abandoned...but always delivered

---

29. De Vaux 1973:110 (quoted in Grogan 2001:99).

and restored to power by the faithfulness of God'[30] and took hope from this that one day a King would come who would inaugurate God's kingdom.

Taking the King David context seriously makes sense of our second problem, the implications of global significance (e.g. 3:6, 22:29-31, 27:3, 118:10-12). On a regional scale, David did indeed have many enemies, whom he had to fight and subdue. He did command armies, fight battles, and win victories.

Only some of the Psalms have the superscription 'Of David'. What of the others? The Old Testament indicates a strong link between King David and the institution of Temple music and musicians. In 1 Chronicles 16:4-6 he appoints some of the Levites 'to extol, thank, and praise the Lord, the God of Israel.' He appoints Asaph and his associates to give praise in the words that later became Psalm 105 (1 Chron. 16:7-36). He appoints many more Levites 'to praise the Lord with the musical instruments' he provides for the purpose (1 Chron. 23:5 and all of chapter 25). There is a strong connection between all the Psalms and David the king, whether or not a particular Psalm was written by David himself. It is no accident that a common umbrella term for the whole Psalter is 'The Psalms of David' (rather as 'Moses' is the umbrella heading for the Law, and 'Solomon' for Wisdom).[31]

Before moving to the New Testament, let us return to Psalms 1 and 2. The strong connections between these Psalms, noted above, suggests that the King in David's

---

30. Christoph Barth, quoted in Anderson 1970:17.

31. See, for example, John Woodhouse, 'Reading the Psalms as Christian Scripture,' p47f in Shead (ed) 2013.

line who will fulfil this promise to govern the world will be precisely the man who delights in the law of the Lord and meditates on it day and night. This is indeed the model of kingship given by God to Moses in Deuteronomy 17:18-20. For all his good qualities, David fails to do this, and most of his successors do not even try. By the end of the Old Testament, we are left wondering if or when the king will come in David's line to fulfil both Psalm 1 and Psalm 2. The Psalms of David show us the sufferings of the rejected king, the intimacy of the anointed king with God his Father, the innocence of the king praying for vindication, and his prayer for God to destroy his enemies.

In a careful study, Bruce Waltke concludes that 'from a literary and historical point of view, we should understand that the human subject of the Psalms – whether it be the blessed man of Psalm 1, the one proclaiming Himself the son of God in Psalm 2, the suffering petitioner in Psalms 3–7, the son of man in Psalm 8 – is Jesus Christ.'[32] Indeed, 'the Psalms are ultimately the prayers of Jesus Christ, Son of God. He alone is worthy to pray the ideal vision of a king suffering for righteousness and emerging victorious over the hosts of evil.'[33]

So let us move to the New Testament and see where these unresolved tensions point.

We pray the Psalms in Christ because of the full humanity of Jesus the King

Outside of Christian circles, the idea that 'Jesus is God' seems utterly absurd. Within some Christian circles, however, the statement 'Jesus is God' is made rather glibly and with little

---

32. Waltke 1981:7.
33. Waltke 1981:16.

thought and depth. Many a child in a Christian home gets the idea that 'Jesus' and 'God' are pretty much interchangeable words, that if 'Jesus is God' then it must follow that 'God is Jesus.' The New Testament teaches that Jesus is God Incarnate, the Incarnate Son of God, God the Son. And the expression 'Son of God' derives first from the covenant title given to the King in David's line (Ps. 2:7). It has a greater and deeper meaning in Jesus, but we must not lose touch with this original meaning. We need to take seriously the full humanity of Jesus, lest we slip into a docetic understanding of Christ, that He *seems* to be human, but is *in fact* God, that His *apparent* humanity is merely a mask for His *actual* deity.

Once we take seriously His full humanity, the door is open to ask the question, 'What would it have meant for Jesus to sing the Psalms?' It is a natural supposition that this pious, reverent, believing Jewish young man would have joined in the prayers and praises of the Psalms in synagogue Sabbath by Sabbath. We know that, 'During the days of Jesus' life on earth, he offered up prayers and petitions with fervent cries and tears to the one who could save him from death' (Heb. 5:7); is it not natural to assume that some of these prayers and petitions used the language of the Psalms? We hear Him saying to the Father, 'I praise you…' (Matt. 11:25); again, it would be surprising if His habit of praise to His Father God was not nurtured, shaped, and fed by the praises in the Psalms. We must remember that, as He grew from infancy through childhood into adult life, He learned to speak to His Father through the scriptures, as the Spirit opened them to His understanding. He had no short-cut to the life of prayer and praise. It is natural to assume that the Psalms formed a large – perhaps even the dominant – part of this training of Jesus' heart.

We pray the Psalms in Christ because of the New Testament testimony about the Psalms and Christ

To suggest that Jesus prayed the Psalms is more than a reasonable surmise; it is confirmed by the apostolic testimony in the New Testament at point after point, as the Psalms are heard on the lips of Jesus. Here are ten examples.

Psalm 22:1 and Matthew 27:46

We begin with perhaps the most famous of all. Psalm 22 begins with David crying out, 'My God, my God, why have you forsaken me?' Jesus cries these words on the Cross, not because He could not think of any other way of expressing His pain, but because all His life the Psalms had shaped His prayers.

Psalm 31:5 with Luke 23:46

In Psalm 31 David expresses his trust in God and includes the words, 'Into your hands I commit my spirit.' No doubt Jesus has expressed His trust in His Father using these words many times during His lifetime; now, on the Cross, He says them for one final time.

Psalm 6:3 with John 12:27

In Psalm 6 David says, 'My soul is in deep anguish. How long, O Lord, how long?' When Jesus says, 'Now my soul is troubled' this is a clear echo of these words; it comes naturally to Jesus to express His distress in the words of the Psalms.

Psalm 16:8-11 with Acts 2:25-32

In Psalm 16, David testifies to his whole-hearted allegiance to the Lord and his consequent confidence that he cannot die and stay dead. No doubt he is speaking genuinely from his own heart; and yet he did die and has stayed dead. And so Peter on the day of Pentecost draws the conclusion that the one who was truly and whole-heartedly loyal to the Lord was not David but David's successor Jesus the Messiah. That is to say, these words that partially expressed David's heart find their full meaning on the lips of Jesus. It is Jesus who can truly say the words of Psalm 16.

Psalm 18:49 with Romans 15:9
Towards the end of Psalm 18, David says that because of the victory God gives him, 'Therefore I will praise you, Lord, among the nations; I will sing the praises to your name.' Writing about the inclusion of the Gentiles in the church of Christ, Paul quotes this Psalm in Romans 15; the implication is that these words of David find their fulfilment when Jesus speaks them.

Psalm 22:22 with Hebrews 2:12
David writes in Psalm 22, 'I will declare your name to my people; in the assembly I will praise you.' This is what the King does when he leads the people in assembly. The writer to the Hebrews explicitly says that Jesus says them: 'So Jesus is not ashamed to call them brothers and sisters. He (that is, Jesus) says, "I will declare your name to my brothers and sisters; in the assembly I will sing your praises."' Again, words spoken by David find their full meaning when Jesus says them.

Psalm 40:6-8 with Hebrews 10:5-7
In Psalm 40 David acknowledges that God desires, not outward sacrifices, but rather a heart devoted to doing God's will. And so he says, 'Here I am, I have come – it is written about me in the scroll. I desire to do your will, O my God; your law is within my heart.' As with the previous example, the writer

to the Hebrews explicitly says that 'when Christ came into the world, He [that is, Christ] said…' and then quotes these verses from Psalm 40. Although the desire was present in David's heart to say, 'Here I am, I have come…I desire to do your will…' the only man who can say these words and fully mean them with every fibre of His being is Jesus Christ.

Psalm 69:9 with John 2:17

Describing his sufferings, David writes in Psalm 69 that, 'zeal for your house consumes me, and the insults of those who insult you fall on me.' David burns with loyal zeal for God's honour expressed in God's house, the tabernacle. When Jesus cleansed the Temple at the start of His ministry in John 2, His disciples watched and pondered. Later, after the Spirit came, they remembered these words from Psalm 69, 'Zeal for your house will consume me.' And as they remembered, they connected the two. This zeal professed, and to some extent shown, by David, finds its fulfilment in the perfect zeal of Jesus. And, just as David's zeal came with a cost, causing him to be – in a manner – consumed or devoured, so the zeal of Jesus would cause Him too to be consumed or devoured, finally at the Cross, when the temple of His body would be destroyed.

Psalm 69:21 with John 19:28-29

In Psalm 69, during one of the descriptions of his persecutions, David says that, 'They put gall in my food and gave me vinegar for my thirst.' On the Cross, 'so that Scripture would be fulfilled' (that is to say, this Psalm), Jesus said, 'I am thirsty' and they gave Him vinegar to drink. Again, the real and historical sufferings of David find their fulfilment when these words express the experience of Jesus.

Psalm 78:2 with Matthew 13:35

Psalm 78 is a teaching Psalm from an Asaphite song-writer. 'My people, hear my teaching,' he begins, and then in verse 2 says, 'I will open my mouth with a parable; I will utter hidden things, things from of old...' which he proceeds to do in a long Psalm teaching Old Testament history. Commenting on Jesus' use of parables for public teaching, Matthew writes that through this parabolic method, 'So was fulfilled what was spoken through the prophet (i.e. the Asaphite Psalmist writing as a prophet): "I will open my mouth in parables, I will utter things hidden since the creation of the world."' The voice of the authoritative teacher in the Psalms is thereby identified with the voice of the authoritative Christ.

Some of these New Testament uses are crystal clear; others are more allusive. But cumulatively they build up a picture of a Spirit-given understanding amongst the apostles that the Psalms are supremely the songs of Jesus.

The Old Testament scholar Bernhard Anderson writes that the New Testament church 'baptized the Psalter into Christ.'[34] It would be more accurate to say that the Spirit enabled the apostles to draw out from the Psalms the voice that had been speaking in the Psalms from the beginning. Far from imposing the voice of Jesus on the Psalms, they recognised the Psalms as the songs of Jesus.

We pray the Psalms in Christ because of the work of the Spirit of Christ in inspiring the Psalms

The fourth strand of evidence comes from the Holy Spirit. When Samuel anoints David as the 'messiah' (the anointed king), the Spirit of the Lord comes upon him, with the result

---

34. Anderson 1970:5, quoting W. T. Davison.

that he can play music and sing (1 Sam. 16:13 with 14-23).
I do not know if the boy David used, as it were, to strum his
guitar as he watched the sheep, and compose songs. Perhaps
he did. But after his anointing with the Spirit, the lyrics
changed. He became 'a prophet' (Acts 2:30). For the Spirit
who had come upon him was not only the Spirit of God,
but the Spirit of the Christ to come. And, as a prophet, he
'spoke of the grace that was to come' to us and, as he did
so, 'searched intently and with the greatest care, trying to
find out the time and circumstances to which the Spirit of
Christ within (him) was pointing when he predicted the
sufferings of the Messiah and the glories that would follow.
It was revealed to (him) that (he was) not serving (himself)
but (us), when (he) spoke of the things that have now been
told (us) by those who have preached the gospel to (us) by
the Holy Spirit sent from heaven' (1 Pet. 1:10-12).

It should not surprise us, therefore, to find the Psalms
that arise out of David's own experience and express
David's own prayers and praises should also point to the
greater experiences and the deeper prayers and praises of
'great David's greater Son.'[35]

We have seen the strong connection between David and
the Temple musicians. We need to note one additional link.
These musicians share with David the same Spirit of God.
Just as the Spirit of God came upon David, so the guilds of
song-writers instituted by David are described as having 'the
ministry of *prophesying*, accompanied by harps, lyres and
cymbals' (1 Chron. 25:1 – and note also the verb 'to *prophesy*'
used of the musicians in vv. 2 and 3). Matthew 13:35 refers

---

35. A phrase from James Montgomery's 1821 hymn 'Hail to the Lord's
    anointed'.

to the Asaphite author of Psalm 78 as 'the prophet.' It is a natural deduction that the same Spirit who came upon David to inspire his Psalms is at work throughout Old Testament history in the inspired Psalm-writers, whether named or anonymous. We shall therefore expect to find in all the Psalms words that express both the experiences, prayers, and praises of the original singers and – at the same time – point forward to the experiences, prayers, and praises of the Messiah whose Spirit inspired the Psalms.

We pray the Psalms in Christ because of the nature of prayer

The final reason is the most deeply theological: God the Father hears prayers and praises only in the name of Jesus Christ His Son. We may expand this in four stages.

By nature, all our prayers and praises are unacceptable to God

It is a foundational truth of the universe that God is 'too pure to look on evil' (Hab. 1:13) and will not hear the voice of sinners. James writes, 'When you ask, you do not receive, because you ask with wrong motives, that you may spend what you get on your pleasures' (James 4:3). He is right; the desires that arise from our hearts are not such that God will hear them. James describes them as spiritual adultery. As one student suggested to me, our natural prayers are like a wife asking her husband if it's ok with him if she spends the night with another man. It is a shocking but realistic analogy, for our natural desires are not for single-hearted love and loyalty to God. Even when our natural requests contain something worthy – as they may do – always they are so mixed with impure motives that a holy God cannot, and must not, hear them.

We delude ourselves if we think God is so ambiguous and tolerant as to listen to the prayers we pray by nature. Dietrich Bonhoeffer put it well when he wrote that,

> this is a dangerous error, which is certainly very widespread among Christians today, to imagine that it is natural for the heart to pray. We then confuse wishing, hoping, sighing, lamenting, rejoicing – all of which the heart can certainly do on its own – with praying. But in doing so we confuse earth and heaven, human beings and God. Praying certainly does not mean simply pouring out one's heart.[36]

There is one, and one only, to whom God listens, and always listens

In John chapter 9, Jesus gives sight to a man born blind. In speaking to the Pharisees later, the man says this: 'We know that God does not listen to sinners. He listens to the godly person who does his will' (John 9:31). He is absolutely right. He is also right to deduce that Jesus has healed him because Jesus has prayed to the Father for this man to be healed, and the Father has heard Jesus' prayer. He rightly deduces that Jesus is 'the godly person who does (God's) will'. If we may put this reverently, Jesus does not heal this man because Jesus is God; Jesus heals this man because Jesus is the man whose prayers are always heard.

This understanding of the miracles of Jesus is explicitly confirmed in John chapter 11, where Jesus calls Lazarus back to life four days after he has died. Standing at the tomb, Jesus publicly says this: 'Father, I thank you that you have heard me. I knew that you always hear me, but I said this for the benefit of the people standing here, that they

---

36. Bonhoeffer 2005:155.

may believe that you sent me' (John 11:41-42). Jesus brings Lazarus back to life because He prays for this to the Father, and the Father hears His prayer. Again, Jesus does not do this because He is God, but because He is the man whose prayers are always heard. It is a remarkable and wonderful truth: there is one man who can pray and always – always – the Father hears and grants His every request.

It would seem that this asking on earth and hearing in heaven has its roots in eternity, in the eternal relations of the Son and the Father, in which the Son asks and the Father hears, always, gladly, unchangingly. Andrew Murray wrote about this deep truth. Within the being of God, he says, there is an asking (the asking of the Son to the Father); all prayer on earth is the outflow from that original asking within the Trinity:

> The prayer of the man Christ Jesus is the link between the eternal asking of the only-begotten Son in the bosom of the Father and the prayer of men on earth. Prayer has its rise and its deepest source in the very Being of God. In the bosom of the Deity nothing is ever done without prayer – the asking of the Son and the giving of the Father.[37]

Because of the Cross, we may pray in Jesus' name

'There is one God, and one mediator between God and people, the man Christ Jesus' (1 Tim. 2:5). One mediator, and one only. Speaking with His apostles in immediate anticipation of His death for them on the Cross, Jesus repeatedly promises they will be able to pray 'in his name' (John 14:13-14, 15:16, 16:23-24). Perhaps the clearest of these is the last: 'In that day (i.e. after the Cross and

---

37. quoted in Sanders 2010:221.

Resurrection) you will no longer ask *me* anything (as they
had asked Jesus during His earthly ministry with them).
Very truly I tell you, my Father will give you whatever
you ask in my name. Until now (i.e. until the Cross) you
have not asked for anything in my name (i.e. you have not
asked the Father for anything in my name). Ask and you
will receive, and your joy will be complete' (John 16:23-24).
Precisely because Jesus is the Lamb who takes away their
sin (John 1:29), His substitutionary atoning sacrifice
means that the prayers of those who are by nature sinners
may be heard; for now they are reckoned as righteous, with
the righteousness of Jesus imputed to them. 'Christians,' as
Fred Sanders has put it, 'are people who talk to God like
they are Jesus Christ.'[38] God listens to Jesus because of His
natural virtue; He listens to us because the righteousness
of Jesus has been imputed to us.

Those who prayed before Jesus came were heard only
because – perhaps in some shadowy way – they trusted in
the Christ who would come. They believed the promises of
God in the covenant, and those promises find their 'Yes' in
the Christ who comes and dies for sinners. Those – like us
– who pray after Jesus has come can only be heard if we pray
on the basis of the atoning work of Jesus for us on the Cross.

Because of the Cross, we have Jesus'
Spirit to enable us to pray
Two great gospel promises accompany the death and
resurrection of Jesus: the forgiveness of sins and the gift
of the Holy Spirit (e.g. Acts 2:38). His curse-bearing
death leads both to our justification and to our receiving
the promise of the Holy Spirit (Gal. 3:10-14). His Spirit

38. Sanders 2010:216.

indwelling the believer enables us to pray. When we pray, this is not our bright idea or simply the overflow of our needy hearts. This is more than what Bonhoeffer rightly described as mere 'wishing, hoping, sighing, lamenting, rejoicing'. It is the outpourings of longings and praises put into our hearts by the Spirit of Jesus through the word of Jesus. That is to say, it is – if it is to be true prayer – the words of Jesus. With deep theological understanding, Bonhoeffer writes,

> true prayer…is the word of the Son of God, who lives with us human beings, to God the Father, who lives in eternity. Jesus Christ has brought before God every need, every joy, every thanksgiving, and every hope of humankind. In Jesus' mouth the human word becomes God's Word. When we pray along with the prayer of Christ, God's Word becomes again a human word. Thus all prayers of the Bible are such prayers, which we pray together with Jesus Christ, prayers in which Christ includes us, and through which Christ brings us before the face of God. Otherwise there are no true prayers, for only in and with Jesus Christ can we truly pray.[39]

The poet George Herbert said that prayer is God's breath in man returning to its birth.[40] When the Spirit of Christ breathed out the Psalms, He gave us the words of Christ to speak by that same Spirit to the Father.

The most concise summary of the biblical doctrine of prayer is found in Ephesians 2:18: 'For through (Christ) we both (Jew and Gentile) have access to the Father by one Spirit.' There are three Trinitarian elements to this. Our

---

39. Bonhoeffer 2005:157.

40. Grogan 2001:109.

access is 'to the Father'; it is 'through Christ'; and it is 'by one Spirit'. Christ's atoning death is the basis upon which we pray. The Spirit is the divine enabling agent of our prayers.

For this most profound of theological reasons we must understand the Psalms as finding their full meaning as the prayers of Jesus Christ.

Conclusion

Putting these five strands of evidence together, it becomes clear that the Psalms are supremely the songs of Jesus. 'The Psalter is the vicarious prayer of Christ for his congregation.'[41]

In his Preface to the Psalter, Luther writes,

> I would rather hear what a saint says than see the deeds he does, [and] would far rather see his heart, and the treasure of his soul, than hear his words. And this the Psalter gives us most abundantly concerning the saints... There you look into the heart of all the saints, as into fair and pleasant gardens, yes, as into heaven itself.[42]

Luther's point is well made. It is a wonderful thing to watch the actions of a believer and to hear their words; it is a still more wonderful thing to look into their heart. But it is even more wonderful when we grasp that within those hearts is the Spirit of the Christ who was yet to come.

In his *Letter to Marcellinus*, Athanasius explains how the Psalms help us more deeply to understand Christ. This is because, before Christ came among us, God 'sketched the likeness of this perfect life for us, in words, in this same

---

41. Bonhoeffer 2005:55.

42. Luther's *Preface to the Psalms*, quoted in Brock 2007:170, see also pp.168-171 and also fuller quote in McCann 1993b:13.

book of Psalms.' If the gospels give us Christ's deeds and words, the Psalms open a window into His heart. And, as we see into His heart, we are given a glimpse of the eternal relationship of love between the Father and the Son. This alone would be good enough reason to read the Psalms.

What does it mean that Jesus is the singer of the Psalms? Signing up for Jesus's Choir

We need now to address an objection. When teaching this material, I am aware that at this stage there is considerable pushback from my hearers. Those who have been disciples of Jesus for many years have grown deeply attached to the Psalms. The Psalms, and some in particular, have comforted them and put precious words and promises on to their lips at times of great sadness and pressure. It seems as if, by this teaching, we are taking these treasures away from them and telling them they cannot pray them after all, or not with integrity. By the time you have gone through, for example, Psalm 23 pointing out the parts that simply do not fit with our experience, pious and devout listeners may be feeling quite cross! 'Why can we not pray the Psalms?' they ask in some exasperation. What does it matter if we have to fudge it a bit and pick the parts that fit and speak to our hearts?

The answer is that it matters a lot, as we shall see. So let us take a step back and consider the model for reading the Psalms to which the evidence leads us. When – as so often – the voice we hear is that of the King or Leader of the people of God, it is natural to hear that voice as the echo of a later and greater voice, of Jesus the King and Leader of the people of God. He it is who suffers so deeply, whose victories have such a great significance, who can claim such innocence, and who has the right to pray for God's enemies to be defeated. Dietrich Bonhoeffer puts it like this:

> The Psalms that will not cross our lips as prayers, those that make us falter and offend us, make us suspect that here someone else is praying, not we – that the one who is here affirming his innocence, who is calling for God's judgment, who has come to such infinite depths of suffering, is none other than Jesus Christ himself. It is he who is praying here, and not only here, but in the whole Psalter….The *human* Jesus Christ to whom no affliction, no illness, no suffering is unknown, and who yet was the wholly innocent and righteous one, is praying in the Psalter through the mouth of his congregation. The Psalter is the prayer book of Jesus Christ in the truest sense of the word.[43]

But we must not stop there. For the Spirit of Christ indwells His church. That same Spirit who drew out of the man Christ Jesus such prayers and praises lives in us His Body (1 Cor. 3:16). We are united with Him by faith. We pray in His name and by His Spirit. Our prayers and praises rise to the Father through Christ by the Spirit. If Jesus is the song-leader, we are the choir, to use a lovely analogy first suggested by Augustine. 'When you sing the Psalms, you are actually singing the songs of Jesus, with Jesus as your songleader.' Rather than listening to a choir of many singers, you are joining the choir. '*His* song is being performed, and the rest join him in singing it.'[44] 'Christ is the great choirmaster who tunes our hearts to sing God's praises.'[45]

---

43. Bonhoeffer 2005:54.

44. Lefebvre 2010:53f.

45. Calvin, quoted in Chester 2005:16.

To say that Jesus is the choir-leader is to build on the Old Testament pattern whereby the King was responsible for the Temple worship, and led the people in prayer and praise. David's song in 2 Samuel 22 becomes Israel's song in Psalm 18. We see this most dramatically as Solomon leads the people in prayer and praise at the dedication of the Temple in 1 Kings 8 but also earlier in Israel's history as Moses leads the people (Exod. 15:1 and Deut. 32:44, the latter with Joshua), followed by Joshua (Josh. 10:12), Deborah and Barak (Judg. 5:1). It is a helpful image to hold in our minds as we pray the Psalms, Jesus our King at the front leading us out in prayer and praise. 'In biblical worship, it is the king who leads the congregation into worship, and it is the king's own songs that the congregation sings with him.'[46]

We must take the Psalms away from anyone who thinks they can sing them as an individualistic 'me and God' thing, as if they are valid outside of Christ. We cannot do this with integrity. There is too much that simply does not fit. It kidnaps the Psalms and places them in the service of a vague and comforting 'spirituality' and must be resisted.

But, after we have insisted on that painful prohibition, the good news is that *in Christ* we may indeed take back the Psalms. In the quotation above, Bonhoeffer concludes by saying, 'the *human* Jesus Christ...is praying in the Psalter *through the mouth of his congregation*' (my italics). As we pray the Psalms, Jesus leads us and we join in, as His choir.

> Jesus Christ prays the Psalter in his congregation. His congregation prays too, and even the individual prays. But they pray only insofar as Christ prays within them;

---

46. Lefebvre 2010:43.

they pray here not in their own name, but in the name
of Jesus Christ. They pray not from the natural desires
of their own hearts, but rather out of the humanity
assumed by Christ. They pray on the basis of the human
Jesus Christ. Their prayer will be met with the promise
of being heard only when they pray on this basis. Because
Christ prays the prayer of the Psalms with the individual
and with the church before the heavenly throne of God,
or rather, because those who pray the Psalms are joining
in the prayer of Jesus Christ, their prayer reaches the ears
of God. Christ has become their intercessor.[47]

Graeme Goldsworthy argues that when we

apply a consistent principle of Old Testament interpretation…we will find that all the Psalms, without exception,
point us to the person and work of Jesus. Thus, as a con-
sequence of this reference to Christ, they point to us who
are 'in Christ' and who are thus defined by who Jesus is.[48]

Augustine was one of the first post-biblical teachers to
make much of this theme. Frequently he cited the Risen
and Exalted Jesus saying to Saul, 'Why do you persecute
me?' (Acts 9:4) to illustrate the corporate identity of the
Church as the body of Christ. Training ourselves to sing the
Psalms as men and women in Christ means that one of the
great functions of the Psalms is to show us what it means
to be in Christ and to settle us there in our affections.[49]
In more technical language, this means that our reading of
the Psalms is both Christological (Jesus is the great Singer)
and Ecclesiological (we the church sing them in Christ).

47. Bonhoeffer 2005:55.

48. Goldsworthy 2003:132.

49. Brock 2007:124,132.

As Augustine would have put it, the whole world is God's possession. What distinguishes 'the City of God' is that it laments and praises with Christ.[50] In Augustine's treatment of the Psalms we find that he 'has provided a suggestive account of the Psalms as standing divine invitations to enter the community of praise.'[51]

There is treasure in the heart of Jesus. The Psalms open a window into that heart. But, as William Gadsby's hymn 'Immortal Honours' so beautifully puts it,

> In him there lives a treasure all divine
> and matchless grace has made that treasure mine.

When we sing the Psalms we celebrate that all the treasure of Jesus is ours by grace.

Question: Can Jesus sing words of penitence and confession?

One difficulty with saying that the Psalms are the songs of Jesus is that they include expressions of penitence and confession, perhaps most famously in Psalm 51, but in many other places. We saw earlier that Hebrews quotes part of Psalm 40 as spoken finally by Jesus Christ. But in that same Psalm, David says 'my sins have overtaken me…' (v. 12). This raises the question: can Jesus say words that admit He is a sinner? Surely if He is without sin, this cannot be possible.

There are two ways of addressing this problem. One is simply to exclude those verses from the songs of Jesus and to say that Jesus only sings the other parts of the Psalms. While this is possible, it is not so easy to cut out words

---

50. Brock 2007:149.
51. Brock 2007:163f.

of confession, which are often rather tightly tied in to the Psalms of which they are part. So, to stay with Psalm 40, the words 'my sins have overtaken me' fall in the middle of verses in which David's sufferings are precisely the outworking of his sins having overtaken him.

A second – and in my view more deeply satisfying – way of coming at this, is as follows. On the Cross, Jesus 'was made to be sin' for us (2 Cor. 5:21); the Father saw in Jesus a sinner bearing in His own body the sins of all His people. Our sin was not just laid upon Him; He became sin for us. The shadow of that terrible identification with sinners fell upon Jesus long before, and certainly from the start of His public ministry. John the Baptist administered a baptism of repentance for sins. When Jesus came to submit to that baptism, John remonstrated that this was inappropriate. But Jesus insisted: 'Let it be so now; it is proper for us to do this to fulfil all righteousness' (Matt. 3:13-15). From the start, Jesus was 'numbered with the transgressors' (Isa. 53:12). When joining in a Psalm in Synagogue, it would be surprising if Jesus stopped singing when the Psalm came to words of penitence. No, despite being Himself without sin, He was so identified with His people that He could lead us in expressing our sorrow for sin, our confession of sin, and our repentant turning from sin. In them, Jesus shows us how closely He 'identifies with us in our deepest need'. In them we know 'without a doubt that Jesus truly does stand with us to intercede even in our repentance.'[52]

In supporting this way of reading, Calvin writes that, 'This was the reason for [Jesus'] silence at the judgement-seat

---

52. Lefebvre 2010:83.

of Pilate, though he had a just defence to offer; [because of his] having become answerable for our guilt.'[53]

Jesus 'speaks in the Psalms as our representative head – our mediatorial king. The Psalms of repentance are no exception to this mediation. Jesus never sinned, but as our mediator, He took personal responsibility for our sins.' Indeed, 'the Psalms of repentance give us precious prayers to' enable us 'to repent in the name of Jesus.'[54]

Some Benefits of singing the Psalms in Christ

I hope I have persuaded you that praying the Psalms in Christ is the true way to pray them, that this is not some arbitrary schema imposed upon the Psalms by the dictates of a prior systematic theological framework. It is not only true, however, but has many benefits. Let us consider how it addresses the five big problems we identified in chapter 2.

We can join in expressions of great suffering, in Christ

Chapter 7 develops this benefit.

We can share in the cosmic significance of Christ

When you and I find ourselves praying words that imply worldwide implications tied up with the struggles and victory of the Psalmist, we no longer need to omit them. Rather, as members of the choir of Jesus, we understand that His battles and His victories do indeed have entailments for the whole people of God and for the world. In His victory is our victory. In His past resurrection is the assurance of our future resurrection. In His exaltation is the guarantee that we will reign with Him (2 Tim. 2:12; cf. 1 Cor. 6:2).

---

53. Lefebvre 2010:83.

54. Lefebvre 2010:87.

We can enjoy our imputed righteousness, in Christ
Chapter 6 opens up this blessing.

We can even pray for God's judgment, in Christ
You and I hesitate to pray for the punishment of the wicked,
because we fear we are praying for our own destruction and
we are apprehensive lest such prayers come from us from
motives mingled with ugly desires for revenge. Vengeance,
we know, can never be ours, for we will always get it wrong; it
must belong to God to repay, for He alone knows the heart
and will judge justly. And yet Jesus, the one who gives His
life for sinners, is the one who alone can pray with absolute
purity and integrity for the final victory of God over all
His enemies. Chapter 8 is devoted to the imprecations in
the Psalms. At this point we simply note that praying the
Psalms in Christ will prove to be the key to including these
in our prayers.

*We can make sense of the singulars and
plurals of the Psalms, in Christ*
When we have in our minds this image of Christ the
choir-leader and us as the choir, the singulars and plurals
in the Psalms fall into place. 'The Psalms of the Bible are
not individualistic poems such as a modern person might
compose to express his own thoughts and feelings.'[55] An
individual Psalmist, speaking in the first person singular,
foreshadows Christ the song-leader. Corporate references,
to the whole people of God, refer to us as Christ's body,
Christ's church, Christ's choir.

   I mentioned in chapter 1 that one of the great blessings
of singing the Psalms in Christ is that it saves us from

---

55. Anderson 1970.

the dangerous isolation of individualism and indeed of idiosyncrasy in our relationship to God. Even if we pray a Psalm on our own, we are joining in the chorus of the people of Christ down the ages. Our prayers are shaped with their prayers by the prayers of Christ. Claus Westermann wrote this about the place of the Psalms in the life of Christian prisoners:

> Whenever one in his enforced separation praised God in song or speech... he was conscious of himself not as an individual, but as a member of the congregation. When in hunger and cold between interrogations, or as one sentenced to death, he was privileged to praise God, he knew that in all his ways he was borne up by the church's praise of God.[56]

Conclusion

Praying the Psalms in Christ does justice to their original meaning and context, to the humanity of Jesus, to the New Testament use of the Psalms, to the ministry of the Spirit of Christ in inspiring them, and to the nature of prayer itself. It is not just one option in praying the Psalms, but rather the true way of reading them.

4. Examples of praying the Psalms in Christ

The idea that the Psalms are the songs of Jesus is an old one rooted deeply in Christian history and − above all − in the theology of the whole Bible. It is nonetheless a sadly neglected truth. For many of us, it involves a massive paradigm shift. In order to help with this transition, I am

---

56. Westermann 1965:10 (quoted in Anderson 1970:2).

going to work through three Psalms of David to show how this understanding works itself out in preaching or teaching many – perhaps the majority of – the Psalms. At the same time I will compare two other strategies that are commonly adopted.

The first alternative strategy, if we may call it that, is to read the Psalm directly to me, so that it becomes my song, and I completely ignore the fact that it was ever anybody else's song (including David's).

A Psalm --------- for Me

The second approach is an improvement, because it takes seriously the original context. I read the Psalm first as David's prayer. But I then translate directly across from David to me.

A Psalm of David ----------- for Me

The third, and best, way of reading the Psalm is to draw the line from David to Christ and only then, not to me as an isolated individual, but to us the people of God, in Christ.

**A Psalm of David, fulfilled in Christ, to
be sung by all the church in Christ**

So let us see how these approaches work, with reference to three Psalms of David.

**Example I: Psalm 3: Praying under
the pressures of Christ**
A Psalm of David. When he fled from his son Absalom.

> [1] LORD, how many are my foes!
>   How many rise up against me!
> [2] Many are saying of me,
>   'God will not deliver him.'

> [3] But you, LORD, are a shield around me,
>   my glory, the One who lifts my head high.
> [4] I call out to the LORD,
>   and he answers me from his holy mountain.
> [5] I lie down and sleep;
>   I wake again, because the LORD sustains me.
> [6] I will not fear though tens of thousands
>   assail me on every side.
> [7] Arise, LORD!
>   Deliver me, my God!
>   Strike all my enemies on the jaw;
>   break the teeth of the wicked.
> [8] From the LORD comes deliverance.
>   May your blessing be on your people.

The Psalm divides into four couplets. Verses 1 and 2 speak of pressure. Verses 3 and 4 point to the promise of God. Verses 5 and 6 affirm personal trust. Verses 7 and 8 are a final prayer and affirmation of assurance.

With the first two approaches, we need to consider which parts of the Psalm need to be fudged, because they do not exactly fit my own individual experience.

1, 2   I'm not sure I have all that many foes. And I've not heard them directly say, 'God will not deliver him.' I can understand that this was precisely David's experience; but it is only sometimes, and approximately, my own.

3, 4   Given that 'lifts my head high' is an idiom referring to military victory, this can only be approximately, or metaphorically, true for me, although it could be David's exact experience. And it is far from clear why I can be as sure as David is in verse 4 that my prayer will be answered!

5, 6   Verse 5 might fit, but what about the 'tens of thou-sands' of verse 6? Again, that could be precisely true of David; but it can at best be approximately true of me, and only with a considerable element of hyperbole.

7, 8a I am not sure quite what it would mean for me to pray this about my enemies even if I knew exactly who my enemies are.

8b   If this is my individual prayer, I am not sure how 'your people' are affected by what happens to me.

So if I am to pray this immediately as my prayer, I have to say something like this.
    From the Psalm direct to me:

[1] (vv. 1, 2) I feel squeezed, under various pressures.

[2] (vv. 3, 4) The Psalm helps me to think God will help.

[3] (vv. 5, 6) I am going to try to trust God to help.

[4] (vv. 7, 8) I pray God will help.

This first approach ought to leave us very uneasy, for it is little more than comforting make-believe.
    If I begin – as I should – with the context of David, I will read it like this.
    From the Psalm via David to me:

[1] (vv. 1, 2) David was under tremendous pressure. I feel rather the same.

[2] (vv. 3, 4) David believed God had promised to help. I hope God has promised the same to me.

[3] (vv. 5, 6) David trusted God. I will try to do the same.

[4] (vv. 7, 8) David prays for God to help. I should do the same.

The weak link here is the uncertain grounds for thinking I can move from David to me.[57]

This is less bad than the first approach, but it should still leave us with a sense of unease, partly because of the fudges that have had to be made, and – more seriously – because I end up exhorting myself to try to follow David's good example. So the end result is often a form of moralising: David did this and that; now you try to do the same.

So let's try taking seriously the original context, in which David is the anointed King. The superscription says he wrote this Psalm 'when he fled from his son Absalom'. We read 2 Samuel:15-18 and immerse ourselves in this terrible and dramatic episode in David's kingship. His handsome, self-centred son Absalom leads a popular rebellion. David flees Jerusalem, crosses the Kidron valley, and faces almost certain death. It is a desperate time for God's anointed king. Let us begin with this original context for each section of the Psalm. In this context the Psalm makes perfect sense.

The King is under terrible pressure (vv. 1, 2)
Notice how the pressure rises with the threefold repetition of 'many'. In 1a the foes are 'many', but static; they just

---

57. One commentator writes, 'So here is David's prayer in trouble. Maybe it's a prayer for you. Let's walk through it, remembering David is the special king but allowing you to nevertheless identify with him' (Davis 2010:40). The problem is that I need some reason for thinking God will treat me the same way He treated David. That reason is found only in Christ.

'are'. At the start of the rebellion a messenger comes to David and says, 'The hearts of the people of Israel are with Absalom' (2 Sam. 15:13). The polls are against you; your personal ratings are at rock bottom; you are on your own; you are heavily outnumbered.

In 1b they are still 'many' but now active; they 'rise up against me' in rebellion. They act on their hostility. In a way, the cosmic hostility to God's king that Psalm 2 so dramatically portrayed (vv. 1-3) is being made concrete in Absalom's rebellion.

But the climax is in verse 2. The worst thing these 'many' are doing is speaking; listen to what they say about me: 'God will not deliver him.' The very worst thing about David's pressures is the suggestion that he might as well not bother to pray, because God will not answer and help him. It is easy to understand why. As David fled Jerusalem, a man called Shimei pelted him with stones and shouted, 'Get out, get out, you murderer, you scoundrel! The Lord has repaid you for all the blood you shed in the household of Saul, in whose place you have reigned. The Lord has given the kingdom into the hands of your son Absalom. You have come to ruin because you are a murderer!' (2 Sam. 16:7-8). Don't bother praying, because God won't hear. If you add in a guilty conscience about Bathsheba and the arranged death of her husband Uriah, the thoughts in David's mind must have made a toxic mix of despair. 'Perhaps they are right; maybe God will not rescue me', he must have thought.

It will not do to move straight from David's plight to my own feelings of being under pressure. David is the anointed King. But if we track forward in Israelite history, we find that David's pressures are in some ways typical of at least one of his successors. At the time of the Assyrian invasion, King Hezekiah was besieged in Jerusalem, surrounded by a huge Assyrian army, 'many' indeed (2 Kings: 18, 19). What is more, these enemies did indeed mock Hezekiah, telling him that God would not rescue him (2 Kings 18:19-25, 28-35).

But we do not stop with Hezekiah. We track right on to great David's greater Son, another and final King who knew what it was to have many foes. The religious establishment was against him. The political establishment was hostile. From very early in His public life 'the Pharisees went out and began to plot with the Herodians how they might kill' Him (Mark 3:6). Finally the occupying imperial power of Rome condemned Him to a shameful death. This King knew what it was to be watched by many hostile eyes, to be plotted against by powerful enemies, and finally to be mocked: 'He saved others...but he can't save himself! He's the king of Israel! Let him come down now from the cross, and we will believe in him. He trusts in God. Let God rescue him now if he wants him, for he said, "I am the Son of God".' (Matt. 27:42-43). No, they said, God will not deliver Him.

And yet we must not stop even there. Verse 8 is the key to understanding where you and I come into the story. The King prays; the King is given victory (v. 8a); and the result is blessing for the people (8b). When the King is defeated, his loyal people share his grief and curse; when the King is delivered, his people experience the blessings that overflow from the King's triumph.

And so, from verses 1 and 2, if the King is under pressure, the King's loyal people must expect to experience something of the King's pressures with him, as David's loyal followers did when they fled Jerusalem with him. This is precisely what the New Testament teaches, that we will suffer with Jesus our King. They may be pressures of temptations – when greedy desires rise in our hearts, or impure thoughts, or resentful bitterness. Jesus knew the pressure of temptation as no other. We too will feel these thoughts and desires swirl around in our hearts and threaten to destroy us. They are the pressures of Christ. They may be pressures of sadness and grief, of sickness and weariness, of discouragement and conflict, of persecution, the sheer difficulty of keeping going as a Christian. These too are the overflowings of the pressures of Christ.

Verses 1 and 2 are not my direct experience, for they are the pressures of the King. But, as one of the King's loyal people, I must expect some overflow of those pressures and not be surprised when I do.

The King has a sure covenant promise (vv. 3,4)

The tone changes in verse 3 from a tone of concern to the music of confidence. From looking around at his 'many' enemies, the King looks up to the covenant God. In the midst of danger, the King sings of safety. He sings to the LORD. He affirms that this Covenant God will be his 'shield' – protecting him from the many foes rising up against him – his 'glory' and the one who 'lifts my head high,' which is an idiom for victory or vindication (as Pharaoh 'lifted up the head' of his cupbearer when he gave him back his job, Gen. 40:13). When David fled Jerusalem 'his head was covered and he was barefoot' (2 Sam. 15:30); the day will come when his head will be held high in triumph.

He calls out in prayer to this Covenant God (4a), 'and he answers me from his holy mountain' (4b). Only the King

David context makes sense of 'his holy mountain.' The pious but unthinking Christian who wants to celebrate that God 'answers me from his holy mountain' needs to give some thought to what this means. Psalm 2 gives a clue in verse 6, where God says to the rebellious powers, 'I have installed my king on Zion, my holy mountain.' This is shorthand for the place of the Covenant with David the King in 2 Samuel 7, the city of David, the place in which the promise to David is focussed. For God to answer David 'from his holy mountain' is for God to keep His covenant promise to David that one of his successors will rule the world, as Psalm 2 affirms. God will not answer *me* from His holy mountain; He will answer *His King*, because He has made a covenant with His King.

It is important to unpack this language. For it makes us focus on the grounds for David's confidence, which are neither his goodness (for he is under judgment for sin) nor his circumstances (for they are dire), but the covenant promise of God to His anointed King, to whom He promised the kingship. This is not a promise for any random believer. 'I have installed *my king* on Zion, my holy mountain' (Ps. 2:6). It is because David is King that he can appeal to the 'holy mountain' as the place that speaks of covenant promise. This promise flies like an arrow through Old Testament history, in spite of the many failures of David and his line. It is the promise that 'You are my son… Ask of me, and I will make the nations your inheritance, the ends of the earth your possession…' (Ps. 2:7-8). It finds its fulfilment in Jesus the son of David.

So, going back to verse 8b, what are the blessings that come to the people? The promise you and I claim in verses 3 and 4 was not made to us. God is not a shield to me, the one who lifts up my head, the one who answers me from His holy mountain. He is all these things to Christ. And then to us, only as we rest in Christ. In Christ we inherit all the promises of God, but only in Christ, to whom those promises were made. If we suffer the pressures with Jesus our King, we will share in the glory of Jesus our King (Rom. 8:17).

The King can rest in those covenant promises (vv. 5,6)
In verses 5 and 6 we move from the affirmation of objective Covenant truth to the subjective enjoyment of that assurance. Surrounded by enemies, engulfed in threats, David lies down and sleeps, confident he will wake again, because the LORD sustains him. With every human reason to fear, he says 'I will not fear' even though his circumstances are unchanged and 'tens of thousands' (the threefold 'many' of vv. 1-2) assail him on every side. Absalom's rebellion is in full flood; and yet David sleeps his first night in the wilderness, and God protects him.

Like the objective covenant promise, this subjective trust flies like an arrow through Old Testament history. Until we watch another King, surrounded by great pressures, claiming His Father's promise, resting in trust. We watch Him in a small boat in a terrifying storm that threatens His life, asleep on a pillow (Mark 4:38). We see Him sleep night by night, despite the many seeking His life. Finally, at just the right time, we watch Him give Himself up to His enemies, sleep the sleep of death, confident that the Lord will awaken Him, as He did on that first Easter morning.

Tracking forward again to verse 8b, the blessings that come to the King's people include the rest of assurance: In Christ, we too may begin to learn to enjoy the subjective assurance that comes from belonging to Christ. We too may begin to rest and trust with Jesus.

The King will experience a great deliverance (vv. 7 and 8a)
David echoes the military cry that was given in earlier days when the Ark of the Covenant went out before the armies of the people of God: 'Arise, LORD!' (e.g. Num. 10:35). He prays for God to deliver him, to strike all his enemies on the jaw, to break their teeth. The primary allusion is to enemies like wild beasts; when their teeth are broken they can no longer devour their prey. There may be a secondary allusion: since the worst thing they did was to speak about David ('God will not deliver him'), perhaps the broken jaw and teeth made their mockery less impressive! The enemies will not have the last word. David will be restored to his throne, as indeed he was. He trusted that God would rescue him, and He did, although the rest of David's reign was in many ways unimpressive and disappointing. So what David is affirming will find its true fulfilment in the career of a later King, mocked, pressured, crushed, killed, seemingly defeated; and yet finally vindicated, triumphing over the evil powers, making a public spectacle of them by His death on the Cross (Col. 2:15). For this King will be delivered, raised from death itself, lifted up in glory, ascending to the Father's right hand, and given all authority in heaven and earth, the name that is above every name.

Our blessing comes entirely from our King's deliverance (8b)
The final line, 'May your blessing be on your people' is not an arbitrary add-on ('Oh, perhaps I'd better pray for the church'). It is intimately related to the logic of the Psalm. When the King is delivered – and only then – blessing will

come to the people. The reason what happens to the King is so important is that our destiny depends upon it.

Because our King endured such pressures, inherited such a sure promise, showed such a wonderful trust, and experienced such a great deliverance, blessing upon blessing will come to us.

In Christ, you and I expect to share in the overflow of the pressures of Christ. In Christ, we claim the covenant promise of the Father to Christ, that He will rule the world. In Christ, we begin to enjoy the restful assurance of all that this promise entails. In Christ, we will share in the final victory of Christ. As we see our Captain holding aloft the trophy, our Commander receiving the surrender of His foes, we rejoice that He has won for us every spiritual blessing in this age and the next.

Review

Praying this Psalm explicitly in Christ takes seriously the original context in the life of David, does justice to the whole Bible story of fulfilment in Christ, and enables us to know the blessings of the Psalm as the blessings won for us in Christ alone.

Example II: Psalm 16: Praying with assurance in Christ

> A *miktam*[58] of David.
> [1] Keep me safe, my God,
>   for in you I take refuge.
> [2] I say to the LORD, 'You are my Lord;
>   apart from you I have no good thing.'
> [3] I say of the holy people who are in the land,
>   'They are the noble ones in whom is all my delight.'

---

58. Probably a literary or musical term.

⁴ Those who run after other gods will suffer more and
  more.
  I will not pour out libations of blood to such gods
  or take up their names on my lips.
⁵ LORD, you alone are my portion and my cup;
  you make my lot secure.
⁶ The boundary lines have fallen for me in pleasant
  places;
  surely I have a delightful inheritance.
⁷ I will praise the LORD, who counsels me;
  even at night my heart instructs me.
⁸ I keep my eyes always on the LORD.
  With him at my right hand, I shall not be shaken.
⁹ Therefore my heart is glad and my tongue rejoices;
  my body also will rest secure,
¹⁰ because you will not abandon me to the realm of the
  dead,
  nor will you let your faithful one see decay.
¹¹ You make known to me the path of life;
  you will fill me with joy in your presence,
  with eternal pleasures at your right hand.

This Psalm expounds the simple truth that desire determines destiny. It focuses our attention on the desires of our hearts. What do you and I 'really, really want' (as the Spice Girls sang)? For example, it has been said that our internet searches reveal a 'clickstream' of desires, needs, wants, preferences. You shall know them by their searches. The advertising industry prides itself in studying the desires of the human heart; and it does a pretty good job at exploiting them.

The problem is that it is very hard to answer the question, 'What is the desire of your heart?' I know the answers I would like to give: I want to live a useful life; I want to be

a good husband and father, friend and colleague; I want
to be upright, moral, selfless, loving. And yet even as I give
these answers, I know it is a long way from the whole truth.
There is a dark underside to my desires that I hope will
remain hidden.

Reading this Psalm simply as my prayer is deeply prob-
lematical, as we shall see. Reading it as David's experience,
to be simply echoed by me, is also fundamentally uncon-
vincing. This again is a Psalm that must be read in and
through its fulfilment in Jesus Christ.

Let us begin by considering the Psalm in its original
context as a prayer of David. David

- begins with a prayer (1a 'Keep me safe...'),
- continues with a reason (1b-8 'for...'),
- and concludes with an assurance (8b-11).

David prays for safety (1a)

The prayer is for safety. As so often in his life, David is in
danger. It is clear from verses 9-11 that he is in danger of
death.

David professes single-hearted loyalty (1b-8)

The reason he prays with such assurance (1b-8a) is – in a
nutshell – because he is utterly and single-mindedly loyal
to the Lord: 'for in *you* I take refuge.' Others may seek
refuge elsewhere, but I seek refuge in You, and You alone.
David expands on this very strongly. 'The theme of having
one's affections centred on God gives this Psalm its unity
and ardour.'[59]

Verse 2a is the headline: I say to the LORD (the Covenant God), 'You are my Lord (my covenant master)'. My

---

59. Kidner 1973-5:83.

will is to obey your will. This is a relationship marked and defined by willing obedience.

It is easy to skim over verse 2b. It is actually a most extraordinary profession: 'apart from you' – apart from You and the gifts that You give – 'I have no good thing.' I never look over Your shoulder, as one might at a party when speaking with someone less than exciting, to see if there is some good thing to be found apart from You. I never think or imagine that there might be some blessing to be grasped apart from what You give me, some sexual delight, some possessions, some fame, some comfort, some success, to be sought over Your shoulder. No, never. For I know that all good things come from You.

Verse 3 addresses the question of whom I admire, the people I really want to be with, to be associated with, to have fellowship with. The answer is, not the celebrities, the successes of my culture, but 'the holy people' (the *Hasidim*, shorthand for the humble recipients of your steadfast love, your *chesed*), the 'noble ones', the men and women who trust You, love You, honour You in their lives, never mind what the world thinks of them. These are the people in whom is my delight. When I come home to my wife and she asks me about my day, I will not tell her with excitement about some famous person with whom I have rubbed shoulders; I will tell her about a real believing man or woman whose faith shone through in their life.

In verse 4 David affirms the flip-side of verse 3. All around him are men and women who 'run after other gods,' who seek fulfilment, success, comfort, pleasure in the worship of idols, man-made gods. But he does not envy them, worrying that they might be enjoying life more than him, finding some ungodly secrets of a happy and successful life. No, he is deeply convinced that their lives will lead to suffering and sorrow. Their sorrows will multiply (an echo of the curse on Eve in Gen. 3:16).

In verses 5 and 6 David uses the language of the Promised Land to declare that he is content with what God has promised him. The words 'portion,' 'cup,' 'lot,' 'boundary lines,' and 'inheritance' hark back to Joshua's distribution of the Promised Land. Each family would be given a portion, chosen by lot, bounded by boundary lines, as their cup to enjoy and their inheritance to keep. The only exception was the Levites, for whom the Lord was their portion (e.g. Josh. 14:4; Deut. 10:9). Lord, says David, I am like those Levites; you alone are my portion. I am happy and content with you and what you choose to give me. At no point is my life tinged with discontentment, with greedy grasping for more, with covetousness of my neighbour's wife, my neighbour's possessions.

Then in verse 7 David claims that the Lord's instruction, His counsel, becomes something he welcomes and inter-nalises so deeply that it becomes the instruction of his own heart at night. He stores up the Lord's words in his heart.

Verse 8a sums this up. The eye in Bible imagery speaks of the desires of the heart. 'I keep my eyes' – the deepest desires of my heart – 'always on the Lord.' He and He alone is the one at 'my right hand'.

So, if we ask David, 'What do you most deeply want in life?' his answer is simple: I want the Lord, the Lord alone. Every good and perfect gift comes from Him (cf. James 1:17). He it is who gives me all I need to enjoy (cf. 1 Tim. 6:17). I never, never look over His shoulder to seek satisfaction elsewhere. If I get water to drink, I thank Him for it. It I get food, I enjoy it as a grace gift from Him. If I have a wife and enjoy her intimacy, I thank Him for her; if I do not, I trust Him for all I need, and am content. I take every blessing as from Him, and seek no other. I have eyes, desires, for God alone; my will bends to His alone; my heart is content with Him alone; my mind submits to His truth alone.

...and therefore David is sure of eternal security (8b-11)
As a result of this purity of his heart, David enjoys a wonderful assurance that his prayer for safety will be answered: 'With him at my right hand, I shall not be shaken.' It is because – and precisely because – David's heart is single, pure and utterly, totally, devoted to his Covenant Lord, that David can be confident of life. His pure desire determines his destiny. This logical hinge-point is the key to the Psalm. If you ask David, 'How can you be so sure of verses 9-11?' he would answer, 'Because of the loyalty of verses 1b-8'. A man who is utterly loyal to the God of life cannot be abandoned to the grave, for the God to whom he is loyal is the God of the living. Jesus said something rather similar in Matthew 22:32, when challenged about the hope of resurrection.

There follows a wonderful gladness: 'Therefore my heart is glad and my tongue rejoices.' The final part of David's prayer is characterised by joyful confidence. Specifically, David is sure that his 'body...will rest secure.' He will not be abandoned to Sheol, 'the realm of the dead'; he will not 'see decay,' which is to say that his body will not decompose in the grave. His confidence is not in some airy-fairy 'spiritual' future, but in a bodily future with bones, muscles, sinews, tongue, heart, blood, brain.

The path on which he walks (11) is 'the path of life,' in which there is joy in the presence of God, 'eternal pleasures'

at God's right hand. Friendship with God cannot be
extinguished by death.

We may summarise the logic of the Psalm like this:
I pray for safety and because I am wholeheartedly devoted
to the Lord, I am confident that I will indeed be kept safe.

Who can sing this Psalm?

It is a lovely Psalm; but who can sing it? If desire determines
destiny, then the acid test comes after the death of someone
who claims to sing it. If a man's destiny is life, if his body
does not decompose, then we may be confident that his
heart loyalty was utterly and purely devoted to the Lord.
But if his body does decompose, then we have to conclude
that, however pious his words and appearance in life, in his
heart there was an ambiguity, a conflictedness, something
other than perfect purity.

This has to be our conclusion with David himself. Even
if we knew nothing of the story of Bathsheba, when David
did indeed seek a 'good thing' apart from the Lord's law, we
would know that David was not utterly pure by the fact that
he died, was buried, and his body decomposed in the grave.
This is the simple logic used by the apostle Peter on the day
of Pentecost (Acts 2:25-32), when he quoted this Psalm and
deduced that it could not finally be about David. But, said
Peter, we testify to a man who died, but His body did not
decompose; for He was raised from the dead on the third
day. This resurrection demonstrates that in the heart of
this man there was a perfect and pure loyalty to God every
day of his life. Until the resurrection, however wonderful
the words and deeds of Jesus of Nazareth, it would always
be possible that He was a very sophisticated and persuasive
hypocrite. But when His body does not see decay, then we

know with absolute certainty, that He was precisely what He said He was and seemed to be.

There is only one man in history who can sing this Psalm with simple and perfect truth, who can pray for safety and be assured of safety, even in the face of death, simply because of His pure heart loyalty to God. The New Testament explicitly tells us that this Psalm is a song of Jesus.

So how can we pray Psalm 16?

We need to admit that by nature we can't

First, we need to face head on that we can't. We must abandon any thought that this is a nice comforting Psalm. For it is not. What the logic of this Psalm says to you and me is precisely *not* comforting; it is that by nature we can have no possible hope in the face of death. We know the misery of living under the shadow of death. As we get older, as desire fails, as our faculties diminish, as we get weak and ill, we feel the shadow of death encroaching on the light of our lives. But our hearts are not pure. Every point of David's affirmation in verses 1b-8 is contradicted by our honest testimony. I cannot possibly claim that in my heart I know that apart from the God of the Bible there is no good thing to be sought or found, that my delight is in men and women who love and trust Him, even if they are despised by the world, that I am deeply convinced that sinful desires end in sorrow, that I am content with what God has given me, that my will is to do His will in all things at all times. Far from it! And therefore I am without God and without hope in the world (Eph. 2:12).

So the first step towards appropriating this Psalm is to abandon all cosy thoughts that it is nice. I cannot put these verses on my devotional calendar – or not without a painfully feeble hypocrisy.

We rejoice that our King's loyalty leads to our blessing
But, second, we draw the conclusion of the New Testament, that in the name of this man, and this man alone, there is forgiveness of sins and the hope of eternal life. When the people were convicted of sin as Peter preached on that Pentecost day, they heard him go on to say that when they submitted to baptism 'in the name of Jesus Christ' they would receive 'the forgiveness of your sins' (Acts 2:38). Jesus does not pray Psalm 16 simply about His own security. In His past bodily resurrection is our future bodily resurrection. When He prays 'Keep me safe' (v. 1), He does so for all who will trust in Him, who will be 'kept' (John 17, Jude 1). Your hope and mine of eternal security, of future bodily resurrection, rests entirely on the perfect pure obedience of Jesus to His heavenly Father. There is no other man in whom our hope has substance; but in Jesus it does. So we will rejoice in the loving obedience of Jesus and be confident because of Him.

This also answers the question of how David could pray such a Psalm. David often makes great professions in the Psalms; Psalm 17 is another strong example. He is not being a hypocrite, a proto-Pharisee showing self-righteousness. No, he is a believer, to whom the righteousness of Jesus Christ is imputed as David trusts in the promises of God, and therefore in the Christ who will surely come. Romans 4:6-8 explicitly teaches this with reference to another Psalm. The righteousness of Christ is imputed to us now; it was imputed to David and all other Old Covenant believers then.

The Spirit of Jesus begins to reconfigure our own desires

Finally, the Spirit of Jesus will begin to reshape our disordered and double-minded desires so that our hearts begin to share the loving loyalty of Jesus to our heavenly Father. We cannot say that verses 1b-8 are true of us. But by the ministry of the Spirit in our hearts they are just beginning to become true. You and I will have mixed motives until the day we die. But a heart desire to know God, to delight in God, to learn contentment in God, to believe that blessing is only to be found in God, to long to obey God, these things will begin to well up in our hearts by the Spirit. In our inner being we will begin to delight in the law of God (cf. Rom. 7:22).

One of the keys to this is to understand that the blessings God gives can only truly be enjoyed when we receive them from His hand. When we seek to enjoy them apart from Him – as though we could two-time God and live a double life, partly enjoying Him and, separately, enjoying good things apart from Him – the result is always sorrow and disappointment (cf. v. 4). The saint's rewards are intrinsic to the saint's desires. If a child is told, 'Practise the piano and I will give you an ice-cream', the reward is separate from the desire to practise. But if a parent says, 'Practise the piano and you will enjoy beautiful music,' the reward is intrinsic to the desire.[60] So, when we learn to love and desire God, our enjoyment of all blessings as from His hand becomes a thing of lasting delight.

The vision of 'eternal pleasures' at God's right hand will be fulfilled when the ransomed church of God share with Jesus their King an unblemished desire for God and delight in God.

---

60. Waltke & Houston 1988:337.

Example III: Psalm 63: Praying
with the longings of Christ

A Psalm of David. When he was in the Desert of Judah.

¹ You, God, are my God,
     earnestly I seek you;
  I thirst for you,
     my whole being longs for you,
  in a dry and parched land
     where there is no water.
² I have seen you in the sanctuary
     and beheld your power and your glory.
³ Because your love is better than life,
     my lips will glorify you.
⁴ I will praise you as long as I live,
     and in your name I will lift up my hands.
⁵ I will be satisfied as with the richest of foods;
     with singing lips my mouth will praise you.
⁶ On my bed I remember you;
     I think of you through the watches of the night.
⁷ Because you are my help,
     I sing in the shadow of your wings.
⁸ I cling to you;
     your right hand upholds me.
⁹ Those who want to kill me will be destroyed;
     they will go down to the depths of the earth.
¹⁰ They will be given over to the sword
     and become food for jackals.
¹¹ But the king will rejoice in God;
     all who swear by God will glory in him,
     while the mouths of liars will be silenced.

As with our first two examples, notice the parts of this Psalm that don't fit directly into our experience or prayers. This is always a good discipline, to go through a Psalm looking for the awkward parts. Here the most obvious are, first, verses 9 and 10, and then verse 11. In verses 9 and 10, David is confident that those who want to kill him will be destroyed; indeed, they will die in war ('given over to the sword') and their bodies will be unburied on the battlefield ('food for jackals'). It is not easy to see how this can directly map on to my expectations or prayers. But perhaps the most significant is verse 11. David's grand conclusion focuses on three people or groups.

(a) *'the king* will rejoice in God'

(b) *'all who swear by God* will glory in him'

(c) 'the mouths of *liars* will be silenced'

When we read the Psalm, therefore, we are to think about (a) the king, (b) the king's people, and (c) the king's enemies. I am not the king (a). The only choice I face is whether to be one of the king's loyal people (b) or to be a liar (c).

We will study this Psalm in three stages.

What does it mean for David to pray this Psalm?
First, we will simply walk through the Psalm listening to David praying it. The context is 'when he was in the desert of Judah,' either the dry area east of Jerusalem and across the Jordan, or the arid region south of Jerusalem, the Negeb. The desert is an outsider's place, a lost place, a lonely place. David may have been there during the long period when he was the anointed but unacknowledged king, pursued by King Saul. Or he may have been there (as in Ps. 3) during Absalom's rebellion. But here he is, an outsider, vulnerable and lonely.

As we listen to his prayer, we hear David's desire, David's delight, David's joy, and David's assurance.

David's desire (v. 1)

David longs for God, 'my God,' the God with whom he is in Covenant relationship. Just as a thirsty man in the desert needs no reminder to seek water, for thirst is an all-engrossing need, so David seeks God 'earnestly' and longs for God with his 'whole being.' This desire for the Covenant God is what gets David up in the morning; it defines his heart and his life. The dry land surrounding him becomes a picture of life without the immediate presence of God. There is in his heart an urgent craving for God.

David's delight (vv. 2-4)

David has 'seen' the invisible God 'in the sanctuary' – that is, the Tabernacle (and later the Temple). Here he has 'seen' the Covenant symbols of God, the altar of sacrifice, the reminders of the Covenant. In particular he has seen in the sacrifices God's provision for his sin, and he delights in this. He has seen all it was possible for a human being to see of the invisible God. He holds these signs in his heart so that, even now in the desert, the power and glory of the God of Israel fill his affections.

In a paradoxical claim, he says that God's 'love' ('covenant love' or 'steadfast love') is better than life itself. This is very strange, for life is shorthand for everything that is good – breath, health, food, drink, beauty, intimacy, laughter, love, and so on. How can anything be better than these? The answer must be that in covenant relationship with God he sees the assurance of the life of a future age, in which the shortcomings of life in this age are no more. What he says points to the hope of a better age. In the desert of his present distress he delights in the assurance of the presence of God. 'It is well with my soul,' he might have sung. And therefore (v. 4) he praises God for His covenant faithfulness and prays ('lift up my hands') for the fulfilment of the covenant promises.

Because God is David's delight, it is natural for him to go on to speak of,

David's joy (vv. 5-8)

Here David speaks of a deep satisfaction in God, like a rich banquet (5), of memories of God that bring him joy even in the darkest night in the desert (6), of a confidence that can sing 'in the shadow of your wings' (probably an allusion to the wings of the cherubim above the mercy seat over the Ark of the Covenant). As he clings to this God, so he is joyful because this God 'upholds' him.

The whole tone of the Psalm is one of delight in God and joy in God.

David's assurance (vv. 9-10)

Finally, David expresses a strong assurance of future victory. One day, he says, my enemies will be defeated in battle. And I will win. We need to understand the political reality: either David dies and they win, or they die and David wins. It is either them or him. And he is sure it will be he who comes out on top. And therefore (11a) he rejoices in the God who gives him this victory.

What happens if we try to sing this Psalm other than in Christ?

Second, it is instructive to see what happens if we try to move from David's experience to our own with no explicit fulfilment in Christ. What happens is something like this.

- David desired God above all others. Do you desire God above all others? Do you really? I don't think you do. If you don't feel bad, I will preach on until you do feel bad. You ought to desire God as David did. So go away and try harder to desire God with all your being.

- David delighted in God's word, in God's provision for his sin, in God's presence. Do you delight in God, His word, His provision for your sin, in His presence? I expect you may do a bit, but you really ought to do so a whole lot more. So go away and work at learning to delight in God a lot more deeply than you do just now.

- David rejoiced in God even during the dark nights. Do you rejoice in God? Well, you say, sometimes I do. Oh, sure, I expect you do. But what about in the dark times? Do you rejoice in God then? Not much? No, I thought not. But you ought to. So go away and follow David's example of rejoicing in God.

- David was quite sure his enemies would be destroyed. Are you sure your enemies will be destroyed? If you are, you are arrogant and perhaps unrealistic; or perhaps vengeful.

When we seek just to walk in David's shoes, this Psalm becomes not gospel but law. It becomes a burden to try to imitate David, or a stick with which the preacher can beat us over the head.

How do we read this Psalm in Christ?

We take seriously the three categories of verse 11. First, the King. David prays by the Spirit of the Christ to come. In his desire, delight, joy, and assurance, we see foreshadowings of a greater desire, delight, joy, and assurance. And so we extrapolate forward from David to see that,

- Jesus desired God the Father above all others. Every moment of His life, He longed for fellowship with His Father. When He could, He spent hours in prayer to the Father. He felt the pain of living in a desert world, the dryness, the thirst for the living God. In the desert literally for His temptations, and metaphorically for all of His life, He entered fully into the experience that David foreshadowed.

- Jesus delighted in God the Father above all others. He loved the covenant promises of His Father, and the covenant love of His Father was to Him better than all the kingdoms of this world and their glory. The delight that David found in the tabernacle, Jesus embodied in Himself.

- Jesus rejoiced in God the Father. Even when rejected and misunderstood, Jesus 'full of joy through the Holy Spirit' could say, 'I praise you, Father, Lord of heaven and earth…' (Luke 10:21).

- Jesus was sure of final vindication. Facing His accusers, He said that the time would come when, 'you will see the Son of Man sitting at the right hand of the Mighty One and coming on the clouds of heaven' (Matt. 26:64). The Son of Man will 'come in his Father's glory with his angels' (Matt. 16:27).

Our King does indeed rejoice in God (11a). And, as a result of His desire, His delight, His joy, and His assurance, we too 'will glory in him' (11b).

- It is not that David desired God, and I need to try harder to desire God; it is that Jesus desired God for me, and I enter into the fruits of His desire.

- It is not that David delighted in God, and I need to try harder to delight in God; it is that Jesus delighted in God for me, and I enter into the fruits of His delight.

- It is not that David rejoiced in God, and I need to try harder to rejoice in God, especially in the dark nights; it is that Jesus rejoiced in God at all times, and I enter into the fruits of His joy.

- It is not that David was sure of final vindication, and I need to try to persuade myself to share his assurance; it is that Jesus was sure of final vindication, and I may be confident that in His vindication lies my hope of final victory.

And so a Psalm that can so easily be taught as a burdensome law ('just try harder to be like David') becomes a wonderful gospel. As Calvin put it, 'our happiness and glory depend entirely on Christ.'[61] He leads us in desire for the Father; He leads us in delight in the Father; He leads us to joy in the Father; He leads us to confidence in final victory. This is His prayer, and it becomes ours in Him.

Conclusion
I hope these three examples of simple prayers of David have helped demonstrate both the how and the why of reading the Psalms in Christ. The 'how' is to begin by taking seriously the original context in the life of David, but then moving forward in Bible fulfilment from David to Jesus Christ, before finally considering what it means for us as the people of the King to join in the prayer in Christ. The

---

61. Calvin 1993, Vol. V, p. 443.

'why' is firstly so that we do not need to fudge the Psalm, skimming over or subtly modifying the parts that do not fit; and secondly, to make sure that the Psalms are prayed as gospel prayers rather than experienced as law, with the impossible burden of trying to imitate the Psalmists by doing the best we can.

This chapter and the last have sought to open up something of the richness of what Jesus meant when He said 'that everything written about me in ...the Psalms must be fulfilled' (Luke 24:44). While 'the Psalms' here is shorthand for the third division of the Hebrew Scriptures (the Writings), this way of speaking reminds us that the Psalms themselves speak deeply of Jesus Christ.

But there is much variety in the Psalter. Not all Psalms find their fulfilment in Christ in exactly the same way; not all are 'the songs of Jesus' in the simple way that our examples have been. In the next chapter we explore how to draw the lines of fulfilment to Jesus Christ in ways that are suggested by the Psalms themselves and which do justice to their rich differences.

5. Drawing the lines to Christ

Drawing the main line to Christ

One of the most important, and yet most difficult, challenges in praying the Psalms is knowing how to pray them Christianly, as part of Christian scripture. Or – in the language we sometimes use – drawing the lines from the Old Testament scripture to Christ. We know in general terms that the Lord Jesus Christ is the fulfilment of all the Old Testament scriptures. But the immediate question when praying a Psalm is: how does this particular Psalm find its fulfilment in Jesus?

There are different answers for different Psalms. We must not try to squeeze all the Psalms on to some procrustean bed of our favoured system. Here is a principle to guide us: let the main line of the Psalm lead straight on to Christ in a way that makes us think, 'Yes, it really was necessary that Jesus Christ and no one else should be the fulfilment of this Psalm. Christ is the One to whom this Psalm points and where it leads us.' By contrast, do not – as it were – drive down the main line of the Psalm and then, near the end, veer off to the side to 'find' Christ.

Let me illustrate this distinction with a couple of examples. First, and perhaps controversially, Psalm 23: 'The LORD is my shepherd.' It is common to read this Psalm and then say, 'Well, in John chapter 10 Jesus says He is the Good Shepherd. So "the LORD" in this Psalm must be Jesus, and I will pray this Psalm about Jesus my Shepherd.' The problem is that there is nothing intrinsic to the Psalm that says it must be Jesus who is the Shepherd here. Jesus the Shepherd has to be squeezed in with a hermeneutical crowbar at the end, from a scripture other than the Psalm; He does not arise out of the flow or content of the Psalm in any way. The thoughtful listener will ask, 'Why must it be Jesus?' And the Psalm gives no answer to that. We have driven down the main road of the Psalm and then made what appears to be an arbitrary detour off the road at the end to say, 'Oh, and by the way, it is Jesus who is the Shepherd; so we can substitute Jesus for God here.'

Instead, we note that this is a Psalm of David the King and there are features of the Psalm that make perfect sense for the King ('for his name's sake' in verse 3, the 'table... in the presence of my enemies' in verse 5, the anointing of His head with oil, also in verse 5). Anointing with oil is 'messiah-ing'; the straight line from David the King runs to Jesus Christ, great David's greater Son, the final Messiah. The LORD, who here is God the Father in heaven, leads and shepherds Jesus His Son, the King, through the valley of the shadow of death to the victory feast in triumph over His enemies. You and I sing this Psalm as men and women in Christ; by His Spirit we are caught up into His darkness and His vindication, and celebrate with Him the wonderful truth that God the Father is our Shepherd and in Christ we lack nothing.[62]

My second example is from a very different kind of Psalm, Psalm 99. This is not a Psalm 'of David' and the only King in the Psalm is God in heaven (v. 4). This is not obviously a song of Jesus; it is a proclamation of the kingship of God in heaven. It is easy, but unpersuasive, to say – at the end of our reading through the Psalm – 'Ah, but I know that all authority in heaven and on earth has been given to Jesus; so this Psalm about the Kingship of God must be about the Kingship of Jesus. I can substitute Jesus for God and it all makes sense.' But there is nothing in the content or structure of the Psalm that necessitates such a conclusion.

When we ask, 'How does a particular Psalm find its fulfilment in Jesus?' the answer will come, not usually from the divine nature of Jesus, but from His human nature. It is not persuasive simply to add in some rough equation of Jesus and God at the end and to say, 'Of course, for us as Christians, we know that Jesus is God, and so we can substitute Jesus for God in the Psalm.' It invites the objection, 'Why? Why

---

62. cf. Doug Green's excellent article 'The LORD is Christ's Shepherd' (https://www.academia.edu/5130978/The_Lord_is_Christs_Shepherd._Psalm_23_as_Messianic_Prophecy), accessed 10th August 2016.

can we substitute Jesus for God? Does the Psalm make this a *necessary* conclusion, or is it not rather arbitrary?'

The only human figures in Psalm 99 are Moses, Aaron, and Samuel (v. 6). We learn in verses 6 and 7 that Moses and Aaron had the priestly function of mediating between people and God, and Samuel, in much the same way, 'called on his name' in intercessory prayer for the people (e.g. 1 Sam. 12:23). All three of them 'called on the LORD' in prayer 'and he answered them' because 'they kept his statutes and the decrees he gave them.' The headline truth in the Psalm is the sovereignty of God (v. 1) and His holiness (vv. 3, 5, 9); this is balanced by the gospel truth of His forgiveness (v. 8), brought about through the mediatory intercession of these great human figures. A direct line from this deduces that we need a perfect law-keeping human mediator (a successor to Moses, Aaron, and Samuel) to pray to such a holy and sovereign God for our forgiveness. We have just such a figure in the Lord Jesus Christ. It is possible to worship at God's 'holy mountain' (v. 9) only because we have the mediator whom Moses, Aaron, and Samuel foreshadowed. Such a line to Christ avoids taking a side-turning off the main road of the Psalm but rather drives on down that main road to see where it leads.

Praising Conversations: voices in the Psalms

Not all the Psalms are songs of Jesus. In the Psalms there is a wonderful variety of voices. As the hymn-writer Timothy Dudley-Smith says, hymns and songs can be celebratory (rejoicing in the saving acts of God), declaratory (rehearsing together some aspect of faith), didactic (opening new insights into truth), hortatory (stirring each other up), narrative (retelling part of the 'old old story'), meditative (helping us to reflect) or petitionary (offering up prayers).[63] If this is true for hymns, it is because it was originally true of Psalms.

In a very helpful chapter of his book *Singing the Songs of Jesus*, Michael Lefebvre calls the Psalms 'Praising conversations.' He uses the analogy of Mendelssohn's *Elijah* oratorio, in which, at different times, the soloist Elijah sings to the people, the people (the chorus) sing to Elijah, and the people sing to themselves. He writes,

> The Psalms are not stories like the *Elijah* oratorio; but they are conversations. They are conversations in which the king is always at the center, mediating our praise. But sometimes, the king speaks to the people in the Psalms. Sometimes, the king leads the people in addressing God. Sometimes, the people sing to the king, or to God about the king, or to one another before the king. The Psalms are full of changing voices singing 'praising conversations' with the covenanted king at the center.[64]

The purpose of this chapter is to highlight the voices we hear, and give examples of how to 'hear' and respond to them aright. But in all these voices, the fundamental truth to grasp is that, rather than the Psalms being an individual matter of me and God, they are a corporate affair, in which Jesus our King leads us the people in relating to God. The picture to hold in our minds is corporate and king-led. As we consider some of the varied voices, it is important to remember that more than one of these voices may be heard in a particular Psalm.

---

63. Timothy Dudley-Smith, 'Hymns and Songs in Christian Worship,' Address to the Pratt Green Trust anniversary in Coventry Cathedral, 28th March 2009.

64. Lefebvre 2010:65.

The Son of God (the King) speaks to God the Father

In most of the 'of David' Psalms and some other individual Psalms, this is the dominant voice; these are straightforwardly the songs of Jesus. As we listen to David the King, or some other leader or representative of the people of God, speaking to God his Father, so we hear the voice fulfilled in Jesus the King speaking to God His Father. (e.g. Ps. 3). We join in by praying this Psalm in Jesus' name. In chapter 4 we saw three worked examples of how you might teach Psalms with this dominant voice.

The Son of God (the King) leads the people (explicitly or implicitly) in speaking to God the Father

Here the Psalm includes plural subjects, led by the King. For example, take Psalm 68. Although this is headed 'of David,' it becomes clear that it is sung by all the people, who praise 'God *our* Saviour, who daily bears *our* burdens' (v. 19), who speak of '*our* God' as a God who saves (v. 20), and again in verse 28 ('*our* God'). Indeed, there is a grand procession of the people of God in the Psalm (vv. 24-27), led – it would seem – by David the King. So David leads the people in prayer and praise. In so doing, he prefigures Jesus the greater King leading His church in prayer and praise. Jesus leads; we join in.

In some corporate Psalms, there is no explicit mention of the King. An example would be Psalm 126. This is an anonymous 'Song of Ascents'. It is corporate ('we... our...our...for us...we...our...'); the people of God sing it together, probably at a time in Israel's history when there was no longer a Davidic king. And yet even then there were leaders amongst the people, whether it be a governor like Nehemiah, a scribe like Ezra, a prophet like Zechariah, or a priest and prophet like Ezekiel. Each leader of the Old Covenant people of God foreshadows the great and final Leader, who is our prophet, priest, and king. Implicitly, if not explicitly, the people of God are always led by a man whose role is fulfilled in Jesus the Messiah. Prayer and praises are only heard in and through Him. We pray these corporate Psalms in Jesus' name, as we pray all prayer in Jesus' name.

God the Father speaks to His Son, the King

This voice is not frequent but, when we hear it, it is of great significance. The three most important examples are

- Psalm 2:7-9 (echoed at the baptism and transfiguration of Jesus[65]),

- Psalm 102:25-27, quoted in Hebrews 1:10-12, and

- Psalm 110 (see Matt. 22:41-45)

When we hear the Father speaking to the Son, we listen with rapt attention and treat the Son with the dignity and honour we hear and know He deserves. As the old hymn puts it, 'Immortal honours rest on Jesus' head.'

God the Father speaks through His Son, the teacher, to His people and/or to the nations

In many of the Psalms we hear the 'upwards' voice of the King, or the people, or the people led by the King, to God in heaven. But in a number of Psalms we also hear a 'downwards' voice of authority, speaking on God's behalf from heaven above. This is the voice of the teacher or prophet. It may be the King who teaches, or some anonymous leader; but whenever a Psalmist teaches, he does so by the Spirit of

---

65. Luke 3:22, 9:35 and cf. Hebrews 1:5.

God and with the authority of God. Sometimes this voice includes personal testimony, as for example in Psalm 37:5-6 or Psalm 73. Often it is straightforward teaching, direct second person appeal, as for example in Psalm 130:7, 'Israel, put your hope in the LORD.'

Psalm 1 begins the Psalter with this voice; it is spoken by a leader or teacher to the people of God, or indeed to any who will listen. Psalm 37 is a sustained example of this voice. 'Do not fret...' it begins and continues with a long Psalm of wise instruction. Another is Psalm 78, which begins, 'My people, hear my teaching...' and again continues with no 'upwards' voice of responsive prayer or praise. In Psalm 32, David speaks to the people, declaring a blessing on those who confess their sin and are forgiven, telling his own story of confession and forgiveness, and exhorting them to submit to His (i.e. God's) instruction.

Other Psalms include this 'downwards' voice mixed in with other voices. For example, in Psalm 4, David speaks 'upwards' in verse 1, 'downwards' to anyone who will listen in verses 2-5, and then 'upwards' again in prayer in verses 6-8.

When we hear this 'downwards' voice of authority in the Psalms, we respond in the same way as we do to the voice of God mediated by the prophets; we hear, we believe, we obey. But there is a particular nuance in the Psalms. At the start of Psalm 78, the Asaphite Psalmist says, 'I will open my mouth with a parable...'; Matthew says this instruction finds its fulfilment in the parables of Jesus (Matt. 13:34-35). Jesus is our prophet, priest, and king; whenever we hear the voice of God through Old Testament figures, we hear the voice that is fulfilled in the authoritative teaching of Jesus. Jesus our King and assembly-leader turns to His church, the assembled congregation, and gives us instruction from

God in heaven. These 'downwards' voices are the voice of God the Father brought to us by Christ the Son our Teacher, His final Word.

The people of God speak about their King

Some Psalms are not spoken by the King, but rather about the King. Here are four examples.

In 1 Samuel 2:1-10, Hannah sings a song prompted by God's gift to her of the boy Samuel. The song ranges far wider than this particular mercy. But the most interesting feature is how it begins and ends. At the start, Hannah rejoices (v. 1) that her 'horn' is 'lifted high' – an idiom for victory and strength. At the end, she prophesies that God will 'give strength to his king and exalt the *horn* of his anointed'. At this stage in Israel's story there is no king. Hannah speaks by the Spirit of God, who is the Spirit of Christ the anointed King, the Messiah yet to come. The gospel sung by Hannah is that God rescued her because God will exalt the horn of His Messiah; it is by the victory of the Anointed King that wrongs will finally be righted, and the world put to rights under its King. We sing this Psalm knowing that the gospel she experienced in part is a shadowy but faithful anticipation of the victory of Jesus the King.

My second example is Psalm 20. In verses 1-5 the people pray *for* the King, as becomes clear in verse 9: 'LORD, give victory to the King!' In verses 6-8 the people are given assurance that these prayers are heard. To pray for the King is to cry to God for a King who will be all that the King is meant to be. But in what sense can we pray *for* Jesus? We cannot pray that Jesus will become perfect, for He is already perfect. But we can pray for His return, when

He will reign on earth and we shall have the King we long for ruling over the whole Created Order. Psalm 20 helps us to do this.

Psalm 45 is my third example of this voice. It is a most unusual Psalm, composed for a king's wedding. Verses 2-9 and then 16 and 17 are addressed to the King, praising Him for His beauty and affirming His great destiny. Here we hear the voice of God leading the people of God in praise of our Bridegroom.

Lastly, Psalm 72 is another prayer that the King will be all that He is promised to be. Like Psalm 20, when we pray this we express our longing that our King will return and rule, bringing blessing to the world.

The people of God speak to the nations
Sometimes in the Psalms the gathered church of Christ turn their voices outwards and call to the nations. For example, Psalm 66 is a partly plural song sung by the people of God (e.g. 'our God' v. 8). And it is partly singular ('I…my…I… my…my…my…me' vv. 13-15, 17-20) as we hear the voice of their (anonymous) leader. Most of it is addressed outwards to the nations: 'Shout for joy to God, all the earth!…Come and see what God has done…Praise our God, all peoples… Come and hear…' (1-9, 16). In these Psalms we hear the public gospel appeal in which the King leads the people in calling to the whole world to 'come' and join in the praise.

There are two responses proper to this voice. First, we must heed it, come ourselves and join in the praise of the God of the Bible. That is to say, we must heed the gospel appeal we hear in this outward voice of summons. But then, second, we are to join in the choir as we sing this appeal; that is to say, we do all we can to make that appeal heard in the world. When a voice in the Psalms calls on the whole earth to praise God, it is an evangelistic appeal.

The people of God speak to one another

My final example comes from Psalm 121. In the first couplet (vv. 1,2) an individual believer says, 'I lift up my eyes…my help…My help…'; the remainder of the Psalm (vv. 3-8) seems to be another voice, or perhaps voices, replying to this believer with words of assurance: 'He will not let *your* foot slip – he who watches over *you*… The LORD watches over *you*…' and so on. Perhaps this is one individual answered by the encouraging voices of the whole congregation; or perhaps one believer answered by one other believer. The voice or voices that answer in verses 3-8 give strong gospel encouragement to the believer who speaks verses 1 and 2. We should surely think of the speakers of verses 3-8 as being led – ultimately – by the 'lead voice' of our King and Teacher Jesus Christ; it is through Him that we hear the voice of comfort.

Summary

It may be helpful to summarise in terms of 'vertical' and 'horizontal' voices (where God is spoken of as higher than us). The 'vertical' voices may be upwards – the Son to the Father or the Son leading the people in speaking to the Father. These are the most common voices in the Psalms. Or they may be downwards, the Father speaking to the Son or through the Son to all of us (the church and the world) with the voice of instruction or warning. The 'horizontal' voices may be the people of God speaking about our King, or outwards to the rest of the world, or indeed to one another for our encouragement. But always the voices bear some relation to the King – whether it be the voice *of* the King or voices singing *about* the King or *to* the King.

In Old Covenant Israel, as the people assembled under the leadership of their king in corporate prayer and praise, these different voices were to be heard. In the New Covenant church of Jesus Christ, these voices are transformed into a richer harmony, as Jesus our King leads us in corporate prayer and praise. As we sing the Psalms we attune our ears to these different voices and join our voice appropriately with theirs.

Part Two:

DIFFICULTIES WE FACE IN THE PSALMS

6. Who are 'the righteous' in the Psalms?

One of the difficulties we faced in chapter 2 was when David and the other Psalmists appear to claim for themselves an innocence which surprises us, and which we hesitate to claim for ourselves. We saw in chapter 3 that this innocence makes perfect sense when the sentiments expressed in the Psalms find their fulfilment in the sinless perfections of Jesus Christ. But how can sinners sing the song of Jesus the sinless one? How can we join in? The answer is because the righteousness of Christ is imputed to us.

Luther's great rediscovery of the old Bible truth that we are justified by grace alone through faith alone came first, not from Romans, Galatians, or Hebrews, but from the Psalms: 'it was by studying and meditating on the Book of the Psalms that Luther was impelled to his remarkable discovery of justification: his movement was from the Psalms to Romans, Galatians, and Hebrews, not vice versa.'[1]

---

1. Karl Barth, *Church Dogmatics* IV.1, quoted in Brock 2007:167.

We meet 'the righteous' at the entrance door to the Psalter, in Psalm 1. There is an 'assembly of the righteous' (v. 5), that is, the congregation or church of the true people of God. They walk a particular 'way' (v. 6), a 'way of the righteous' that is lovingly watched over by God. They are the opposite of 'the wicked'. They delight in the law of the LORD; they meditate on it day and night. So who are these people?

As we read through the Psalms there is a puzzling distinction between a righteousness that belongs to God and a righteousness that belongs to the Psalmists. So in Psalm 5 the prayer is, 'Lead me, LORD, in *your* righteousness' (v. 8). In Psalm 143 David calls on the LORD to hear his prayer, his cry for mercy, on the basis of '*your* faithfulness and righteousness' (v. 1) because 'no one living is righteous before you.' So no human being has a natural righteousness before God. Instead he casts himself on what Luther would later call an 'alien' righteousness, a righteousness of God whereby God keeps His covenant promise (hence also 'faithfulness') by doing the right thing and rescuing David His covenant King.

And yet at other times the Psalmists can refer to their own righteousness. For example, in Psalm 18, David celebrates that God has 'dealt with me according to *my* righteousness, according to the cleanness of my hands'; because 'I have been blameless before him and have kept myself from sin' the LORD 'has rewarded me according to *my* righteousness...' (Ps. 18:20-24). In Psalm 7, David combines the two. On the one hand he prays, 'Vindicate me, LORD, according to *my* righteousness...*my* integrity' (v. 8); on the other he thanks the LORD 'because of *his* righteousness' (v. 17). In Psalm 35 David prays, 'Vindicate me in *your* righteousness' (v. 24). So there is a righteousness that belongs to God, which expresses God's faithfulness to His covenant with His King, and yet which somehow becomes a righteousness claimed by the King himself. 'Your righteousness' can become 'my righteousness' in David's life.

That is to say, the righteousness of God is more than simply God doing the right thing; it is a status conferred upon David that can enable him to claim this righteousness as his own. This is a righteousness reckoned, imputed, counted as David's. The flip side of this imputation is that David's sin is not reckoned, imputed, counted against him. David proclaims this blessing in Psalm 32:2 ('Blessed is the one whose sin the LORD does not count against them…'). Paul teaches in Romans 4 that the righteousness David experienced and declares is the same righteousness experienced by Abraham in Genesis 15:6: 'Abraham believed God, and it was credited to him as righteousness' (Rom. 4:1-8). Furthermore, this imputed righteousness is given to all who will trust in the atoning death of Jesus, so that their sins are counted against Jesus and Jesus' righteousness is reckoned to be theirs. This makes sense of our puzzlement when we see David, and other flawed Psalmists, claiming innocence and pleading for vindication. They are not proto-pharisees exhibiting an ugly self-righteousness. Rather, in believing the covenant promises of God, they are trusting in the Christ to come, in whom all those covenant promises are 'yes' (2 Cor. 1:20).[2]

We too can now protest our innocence as we pray these parts of the Psalms without feeling we are pharisaical

---

2. For a concise summary of what 'righteousness' means, see Ash 2009:64-66.

hypocrites exhibiting a terrible self-righteousness. Our
choir-leader protests His innocence with an absolutely
clear conscience; He is indeed without sin; no one can ever
convict Him of sin (John 8:46). And – most wonderfully
– His righteousness is reckoned or imputed to us by grace
alone. In Christ we can even pray for vindication or justice
(Ps. 17:2), since as forgiven sinners we know that God will
be just to forgive us our sins (1 John 1:8-9) and will give us
'justice' when Jesus returns (Luke 18:8).

But there is more to the portrait of 'the righteous' than
imputed righteousness. David claims an actual change in
his life. He speaks of 'the cleanness of my hands' and 'my
integrity' (Ps. 18:20-24 and Ps. 7:8). Psalm 37 says, 'The
wicked borrow and do not repay, but the righteous give
generously' (v. 21); there is a change in the way they handle
their money. Psalm 106 declares, 'Blessed are those who
act justly, who always do what is right' (v. 3, literally 'do
righteousness'). These are not men and women with a ticket
of righteousness in their pockets; they are beginning to walk
in 'the way of the righteous'(Ps. 1:6). Their lives are different.

But could this still be a form of moralism? One more
motif in the Psalms will help to guard us against this
misunderstanding. The righteous are repeatedly said to be
those who 'take refuge' in God. Psalm 5 exhorts, 'let all who
take refuge in you be glad...those who love your name...
Surely, LORD, you bless the righteous...' (vv. 11-12). The
righteous enjoy the blessing of God as they love His name
and take refuge in Him. This is a far cry from Pharisaical
self-confidence. In Psalm 52 the righteous are contrasted
with 'the man who did not make God his stronghold but
trusted in his great wealth' (v. 7); the problem with the
wicked is misplaced faith, and the secret of the righteous

person's blessing is his well-directed faith; he or she makes God their refuge. The righteous, far from being smug or self-satisfied, are men and women under great pressure (e.g. Ps. 94:21), who 'cry out, and the LORD hears them'; they are the 'broken-hearted' to whom the LORD is 'close' (Ps. 34:17-18). This is the language of life-changing faith.

We saw, in our exposition of Psalm 63 in chapter 4, that praying the Psalms in Christ guards against moralism. When we take a Psalm and seek to make it our own prayer as isolated individuals, too often the result can be a religion of law, in which we are being exhorted to praise better, to be more whole-hearted in our love, or – one way or another – to be better and more pious people. But when Christ is our choir-leader, it is He who has done all things well; our calling is not to lead the Psalm and fulfil all the exhortations of the Psalm, but to join in the chorus in Christ. As we do that, we will indeed find our hearts beginning to be changed; but they will be changed by the grace of the gospel, rather than beaten up by the terrors or impossible challenges of law.

Example: Psalm 32

Let us consider Psalm 32 to illustrate the theme of the righteous in the Psalms. Traditionally, this is one of the so-called 'penitential Psalms' to be said or sung at the start of Lent. It may seem surprising to take a penitential Psalm, a Psalm that models confession and repentance, as a worked example to illustrate the Psalms' portrait of the righteous. But notice how Psalm 32 ends: 'Rejoice in the LORD and be glad, you righteous...' (v. 11). This is a Psalm to be prayed by the 'righteous.' And it ends with God's righteous people being filled with joy. Yet it begins with confession and penitence!

David begins with declaring a surprising blessing (vv. 1-2), continues with his own honest testimony (vv. 3-5) and concludes with a gospel invitation (vv. 6-11).

A surprising blessing

> Of David. A *maskil*.
> ¹ Blessed is the one
>   whose transgressions are forgiven,
>   whose sins are covered.
> ² Blessed is the one
>   whose sin the LORD does not count against
>   them
>   and in whose spirit is no deceit.

David declares that the happiest people in the world are forgiven people, because only forgiven people can have fellowship with God. He uses three words for sin – transgressions (crossing the line), sins (getting it wrong, missing the mark), and sin (a different word in v. 2, translated 'iniquity' in v. 5, getting God's straight way twisted or distorted). And he uses three words for forgiveness – forgiven (lifted, taken away), covered (covered up, never to be uncovered, as Abel's blood was uncovered and cried out for justice against Cain in Gen. 4), and not counted (not imputed, not reckoned, not listed on the charge-sheet).

But the surprise is in verse 2b: 'and in whose spirit is no deceit'. If God is to cover up your sin, you need to uncover it, to stop pretending, to stop just being sorry for the bad consequences of your sin. This is exactly what King Saul failed to do (read 1 Sam. 15, in which Saul is forever trying to cover up) and what King David did do after his terrible sin with Bathsheba (2 Sam. 12:13).

An honest testimony

In verses 3-5 David tells the story of how he abandoned deceit and confessed his sin.

> [3] When I kept silent,
>   my bones wasted away
>   through my groaning all day long.
> [4] For day and night
>   your hand was heavy on me;
>   my strength was sapped
>   as in the heat of summer.

It was sheer misery for David to have a guilty conscience, even if he managed not to get publicly exposed for his sin. Those who know the misery of hidden sin will understand his story. It affects not only the mind, but the body.

> [5] Then I acknowledged my sin to you
>   and did not cover up my iniquity.
> I said, 'I will confess
>   my transgressions to the LORD.'
> And you forgave
>   the guilt of my sin.

The moment he comes out in the open before God in confession, at that very moment God forgives. All three sin words reappear (iniquity, transgressions, sin). The forgiveness is as complete as the sin was serious, and as immediate as the confession is spoken; 'The word of confession is scarcely in his mouth, before the wound is healed.'[3]

Either David covers up his sin, or God covers up his sin. He – and we – cannot have it both ways. The moment David stops his own cover up, God does His forgiving cover up.

---

3. Augustine on Psalm 32.

We have seen from Romans 4 that the reason God could be both just and the one who justifies the ungodly is because in one great and terrible future day a guiltless man would become sin for David and bear David's sin in His own body on the Cross.

A gospel invitation

And so David finishes the Psalm with a sustained gospel invitation.

> [6] Therefore let all the faithful pray to you (that is,
>   pray in open confession)
>   while you may be found;
>   surely the rising of the mighty waters
>   will not reach them.
> [7] You are my hiding-place;
>   you will protect me from trouble
>   and surround me with songs of deliverance.

If you believe the message of the King, you too will pray in open confession, in the day of gospel opportunity, 'while (God) may be found'. The 'mighty waters' of just judgment will not reach you in the future; you will be rescued from the death and destruction that is God's righteous judgment against sinners. You too will find, as David did, that God will be your hiding-place on the day of judgment.

And you will walk in fellowship with God in the present. David exhorts the people of God to carry on with the life of penitence and faith:

> [8] I will instruct you and teach you in the way you
>   should go;
>   I will counsel you with my loving eye on you.
> [9] Do not be like the horse or the mule,
>   which have no understanding

> but must be controlled by bit and bridle
> > or they will not come to you.

God is able to make you do what He wants by – as it were – putting a bit in your mouth and a bridle on your head. You can be as obstinate as a horse or mule (cf. Prov. 26:3), but you cannot not do what God directs. But what a miserable way to do it:

> [10] Many are the woes of the wicked,
> > but the LORD's unfailing love
> > surrounds the one who trusts in him.

To heed God's loving counsel, to listen to His word, to live the life of daily confession, daily repentance, daily faith, is to be surrounded by the Lord's unfailing covenant love. And it leads in the end to joy:

> [11] Rejoice in the LORD and be glad, you righteous;
> > sing, all you who are upright in heart!

And so the Psalm that began with a declaration of blessing, but continued with a story of misery, ends with great joy as sin is confessed and the sinner walks again in the way of the righteous.

In this Psalm we hear the voice of a sinful king, David, who found forgiveness and preached the gospel so that others might rejoice in that forgiveness too. And yet, behind the voice of David the sinner, we hear the tones of Jesus our sinless King, who bore our sin for us, who leads us in confession, who declares to us the blessing and joy of the forgiveness He won for us.

To be righteous in the Psalms is not to be self-righteous or hypocritical. It is to love God, to love Jesus, to take refuge in God and rejoice in the forgiveness won for us by

Jesus and the righteousness given to us by Jesus. And it is to have our hearts worked upon so deeply by the Spirit of Jesus that we begin to walk the way of the righteous in a life being changed by grace.

7. How can we pray Psalms of suffering?

In Part One, the first difficulty we noted with our singing the Psalms was the intensity of suffering they not infrequently experience. I took as an example these words from Psalm 88: 'I am overwhelmed with troubles and my life draws near to death…I am set apart with the dead, like the slain who lie in the grave…You have taken from me my closest friends and have made me repulsive to them. I am confined and cannot escape… From my youth I have suffered and been close to death; I have borne your terrors and am in despair…' (from vv. 3, 5, 8, 15)

The sufferings that feature in the Psalms are real and historical expressions of the actual sufferings of David and the other Psalmists. We must take this historicity seriously. And yet the descriptions are infused, again and again, with an intensity that points forward to the Cross of Christ. When we struggle to see how a Psalmist can enter such depths, we understand that the Spirit of Christ gave to their sufferings an intensity that foreshadowed the Cross (rather as we see repeatedly in the sufferings of Job[4]). These sufferings, in all their terrible darkness, make perfect sense when fulfilled in the sufferings of Jesus. But that still leaves the question, what does it mean in practice for us to sing these sufferings as men and women in Christ?

---

4. see Ash 2014.

The answer lies along the following lines. If the sufferings of Christ were foreshadowed in the lives of David and the other Psalmists, these same sufferings overflow today in the pains and trials of Christian believers the world over. Paul writes of filling up in his flesh 'what is still lacking in regard to Christ's afflictions, for the sake of his body, which is the church' (Col. 1:24). We are co-heirs with Christ, 'if indeed we share in his sufferings in order that we may also share in his glory' (Rom. 8:17).

So when I find myself praying words that speak of a suffering deeper than my own, I no longer feel I have to omit those verses. Rather, I speak them as a member of the choir of Christ, conscious that these were His sufferings, and that even today they are overflowing in the sufferings of Christian brothers and sisters the world over, especially in the persecuted church. Sometimes I will find an echo in my own present experience. But it doesn't matter if I don't, for I am praying these words as a member of the worldwide church of Christ.

We will take as an example, Psalm 88. Derek Kidner writes, 'There is no sadder prayer in the Psalter.'[5] We will take it as an example, to see what praying it in Christ means, and feels like, in practice. For if we can learn to pray this dark Psalm, we can perhaps learn to pray the sufferings in all the Psalms.

Worked Example: Psalm 88

The Psalm comes in Book 3 which has a theme of Exile. It comes from Heman, a member of 'the sons of Korah.' Either exile, or the fragile life of the people of God after exile, gives it its flavour. Although an individual sings this,

---

5. Kidner 1973-5:316.

it seems likely that he was leading the people in a corporate lament.

Like so many laments, and like human experience under pressure, the Psalm goes round and round with its themes. The Psalm is punctuated, however, by three clear markers of prayer, in verses 1 and 2, then in verse 9, and finally in verse 13.

As we walk through the Psalm with this sufferer, we shall see four motifs interwoven:

- the persistence of his prayer, (1 and 2, 9bc, 13)

- the depths of his suffering, (3-5a, 9a, 15, 18)

- the agony of his God-forsakenness, (5b-8, 16 and 17)

- the perplexity of his faith. (10-12, 14)

We begin with the persistence of his prayer and a surprising indicator of his faith.

> ¹ LORD, you are the God who saves me;
>   day and night I cry out to you.
> ² May my prayer come before you;
>   turn your ear to my cry.

The Psalm begins with an address that will be surprising and puzzling as we read on. He calls the LORD, the Covenant God, 'the God who saves me' (lit. 'The God of my salvation'). '[T]he Psalm will be all about whether this declaration is true.'[6] It is a striking affirmation of faith right at the start.

What follows is urgent, persistent prayer, 'day and night', and emphasised by the repetition of the theme: '… cry out…my prayer…my cry'.

---

6. Goldingay.

Verses 3-9a begin with 'I...my...I...I...I...' (3-5a) and then move to 'you... your... You... Your... you... your... You...' (5b-9a). Verses 3-5 describe, and help us to feel, the depth of his suffering.

> ³ I am overwhelmed with troubles
>   and my life draws near to death (Sheol).
> ⁴ I am counted among those who go down to the pit;
>   I am like one (a man) without strength.
> ⁵ I am set apart with the dead,
>   like the slain who lie in the grave,...

He is 'overwhelmed,' full to bursting 'with troubles.' Here is a moving description of overwhelming suffering. This great sea of disaster brings him closer and closer to death. Notice the repeated words for death: Sheol (3b), which is the 'not land,' the land that isn't a land. Then 'the pit', 'the dead,' 'the slain' (in battle), and 'the grave'. 'The breath of approaching death drifts through every line.'[7] Don't skim over this; we need to say these lines (as all the other lines) aloud, to feel the distress. Like the demoniac in Mark 5:2, this man virtually lives in the tombs; he might as well be dead already. The shadow of death lies heavily upon him. He is overwhelmed, utterly devoid of strength with which to help himself.

But the experience of deep suffering is not the worst. From verse 5b to verse 9a the focus shifts from 'I/me' to 'You,' from my subjective experience of impending death to You, the Covenant God, and Your role in what is happening to me.

> ...whom you remember no more,
>   who are cut off from your care (lit. your hand).

_____

7. Kraus.

> [6] You have put me in the lowest pit,
>   in the darkest depths.
> [7] Your wrath lies heavily on me;
>   you have overwhelmed me with all your
>   waves.
> [8] You have taken from me my closest friends
>   and have made me repulsive to them.
> [9] I am confined and cannot escape;
>   my eyes are dim with grief.

The worst thing for this believer is that he is 'cut off from your care'. It is not just that he is in the pit and the darkness; it is that 'You,' the covenant God, have put me there. Rather than being the recipient of Your covenant love, I am under Your 'wrath,' which lies heavy upon me, like an unbearable burden. The 'waves' of Your floodwaters of judgment sweep over me; I am drowning. 'One after another, new terms denote the unfathomable depth of Godforsakenness and the experience of death.'[8] Several commentators note the similarity to the start of Psalm 22, 'My God, my God, why have you forsaken me?'

And not only have You cut me off from You; You have also cut me off from the friendship and support of those formerly close to me (v. 8). The effect of my suffering is to make me utterly disgusting, so that they shrink from me in horror at the ugliness that is me. And I am left so desperately alone, imprisoned, 'confined,' (8b), cut off from God, cut off from human love and friendship. My 'eyes,' – which speak in Bible language of ambition, desire, hope, what gets me up in the morning – are 'dim with grief.' I am scarcely alive, and there seems no point in going on living.

---

8. Kraus.

But still he prays. In the midst of the depths of his sufferings and the agony of his Godforsakenness, he persists in prayer:

> I call to you, LORD, every day;
>> I spread out my hands to you.

Again, note the way the intensity of the prayer is emphasised by the different expressions – 'call to you… spread out my hands to you'. And his persistence – 'every day'.

A new note is sounded in verses 10-12. The sufferer asks a series of parallel, and seemingly innocuous, questions that go to the heart of his plea:

> [10] Do you show your wonders to the dead?
>> Do their spirits rise up and praise you?
> [11] Is your love declared in the grave,
>> your faithfulness in Destruction (Abaddon)?
> [12] Are your wonders known in the place of
>> darkness,
>>> or your righteous deeds in the land of
>>>> oblivion?

Here is the perplexity of faith. He knows that the God who saves (v. 1) works 'wonders' (often creation and, here, redemption), that He shows 'love' (that is, *chesed*, covenant steadfast love) and 'faithfulness' to His covenant promises, that He works 'righteous deeds'. All this needs to be praised (10b), but cannot and will not be praised by dead people. The word 'spirits' means something like 'shades' or 'ghosts' and refers, not to spirits separate from dead people, but to the whole of a dead person in their deadness. It is not that they live in some other sphere, and their ghosts come to haunt us; it is that their ghosts are all they are, all that is left of them.

The logic of this part of the lament is very important. He speaks as a worshipper, a man on whose lips is praise for the God who saves, the God who works wonders, the God who is faithful and unchangingly loving, who works in righteousness. If he – one who praises God – is silenced, then God will be praised less; and how can that possibly be a good thing? For it would count against the glory and honour of God. His plea is based not ultimately on his own desperation (though that is intense) but on the glory of God. This is faith – for he knows the God who saves – but it is perplexed faith.

The entailment of these agonised questions is that his present sufferings cannot be the end of the story. His life cannot end in this way, full stop. Derek Kidner draws out the implications of these questions: 'the Psalmist's indignant questions allow no satisfying answer short of (resurrection).'[9] For the God to whom he is joined by covenant is the God of the living, not of the dead (cf. Matt. 22:32).

And so he prays yet again:

> [13] But I cry to you for help, LORD;
>   in the morning my prayer comes before you.

Persistence, alongside intensity, is the theme of his prayers. They are 'day and night' (v. 1), 'every day' (v. 9) and 'in the morning' (v. 13). They have to be persistent, because there is no answer. Although he prays 'in the morning,' morning never seems to come, in any meaningful sense (cf. Ps. 130:5-6).

Finally, in verses 14-18 he reprises his themes of suffering, God-forsakenness, and perplexity.

---

9. Kidner.

¹⁴ Why, LORD, do you reject me
    and hide your face from me?
¹⁵ From my youth I have suffered and been close to
        death;
    I have borne your terrors and am in despair.
¹⁶ Your wrath has swept over me;
    your terrors have destroyed me.
¹⁷ All day long they surround me like a flood;
    they have completely engulfed me.
¹⁸ You have taken from me friend and neighbour –
    darkness is my closest friend.

The question 'Why?' sums up the perplexity. Why should the faithful covenant God turn His face away from a believing, praising man? The agony of Godforsakenness is intensified still further – if that is possible – by the repeated phrase 'your terrors'. On top of pain and weakness, there is a terrified and paralyzing fear. Again, the language of floodwaters is used, engulfing him (17). Again, his loneliness is vocalised (18); indeed, it is with loneliness and darkness that this Psalm ends.

How can we join in such a dark Psalm?

So we come back to our question at the start: how can you and I join in such a prayer, so that it becomes our own, and we move from being hearers to singers in the choir?

First, we find ourselves identifying sympathetically with the genuine and deep suffering of this Old Testament believer, and all Old Testament believers who sang this Psalm with faith and perplexity in their hearts. But the sheer intensity pushes us forwards to the fulfilment of all their sufferings in the passion of Jesus Christ. With good reason, the Book of Common Prayer sets this as the Psalm for Good Friday. 'The Passion of our Lord is here prophesied.'[10] As we listen to Jesus singing this Psalm we gain a deeper insight into the sheer agony of His sufferings; the Psalm gives us a window into His soul. We find ourselves more deeply thankful than before, for all He suffered for us.

But we must go further. If we must suffer with Him before sharing in His glory (Rom. 8:17) and the sufferings of Christ have an overflow into the lives of His church, 'just so in this song of the Passion, Christ going before is followed by the choir of martyrs', where the word 'martyrs' includes not only those who physically die for Christ, but all who are 'imitators of Christ's Passion.'[11] With some echoes in our own lives, and many more echoes in the lives of the persecuted church, we sing this Psalm. The darkness with which it ends presses home to us the possibility of lifelong suffering with no alleviation in this age; not every Psalm ends with morning having broken in the life of the Psalmist.

But even where there is unending suffering in this age, the faithful covenant love of God to us in Jesus Christ means that this cannot be the end of the story. Claus Westermann, in his work on *Praise and Lament in the Psalms*, observes that, 'There is no petition, no pleading from the depths, that did not move at least one step (in looking back to God's earlier saving activity or in confession of confidence) on the road to praise.'[12] Although John Goldingay suggests that Psalm 88 seems to be an exception,[13] I think Westermann is right even here. For the Psalmist's persistence in prayer, his address to God as 'the God who saves me' and the

<hr>

10. Augustine.

11. Augustine.

12. Westermann 1981:154.

13. Goldingay 2006-8:644.

qualities of God in his questions in verses 10-12 are all first steps that will finally issue in praise.

Just as there had to be resurrection for Christ, so there will most certainly be resurrection for all His suffering people. In this dark Psalm, 'the Spirit of God...has... furnished us with a form of prayer for encouraging all the afflicted who are...on the brink of despair....'[14] Let us learn to join in, and to keep it as a precious part of the armoury of prayer that God has given us.

8. Can we pray for God's judgment on the wicked?[15]

The problem

We turn now to one of the most difficult problems we face when learning to pray the Psalms. Again and again, the Psalmists pray for God to destroy the wicked. Here are some examples:

> Pour out your wrath on them;
> let your fierce anger overtake them.
> May their place be deserted;
> let there be no one to dwell in their tents.
> ...
> Charge them with crime upon crime;
> do not let them share in your salvation.
> May they be blotted out of the book of life
> and not be listed with the righteous. (Ps. 69:24-28)

> But may sinners vanish from the earth
> and the wicked be no more. (Ps. 104:35)

---

14. Calvin.

15. I owe a great debt in this chapter to a Teaching Day by the Revd. Andrew Saville given for the Proclamation Trust in 2002, and for the kind loan of Saville's notes, used with permission.

When he is tried, let him be found guilty,
and may his prayers condemn him.
May his days be few;
may another take his place of leadership.
May his children be fatherless
and his wife a widow.
May his children be wandering beggars;
may they be driven from their ruined homes…
   (Ps. 109:7-10)

Daughter Babylon, doomed to destruction,
happy is the one who repays you
according to what you have done to us.
Happy is the one who seizes your infants
and dashes them against the rock. (Ps. 137:8-9)

If only you, God, would slay the wicked!
Away from me, you who are bloodthirsty!
They speak of you with evil intent;
your adversaries misuse your name.

Do I not hate those who hate you, LORD,
and abhor those who are in rebellion against you?
I have nothing but hatred for them;
I count them my enemies. (Ps. 139:19-22)

These are shocking words. And there are plenty more examples of these kinds of prayers in the Psalms. But are we meant to join in praying them? 'Surely not!' we exclaim in horror. It seems to contradict so much of the New Testament teaching.

After all, Jesus taught us, in the Sermon on the Mount,

You have heard that it was said, 'Love your neighbour and hate your enemy.' But I tell you, love your enemies and pray *for* those who persecute you… (Matt. 5:43-44).

As He was crucified, Jesus Himself did this, praying,

> Father, forgive them, for they do not know what they are
> doing (Luke 23:34).

Stephen, the first martyr, followed the Lord's example, praying as he was stoned,

> Lord, do not hold this sin against them (Acts 7:60).

Paul teaches,

> Bless those who persecute you; bless and do not curse
> (Rom. 12:14).

And he sets an example of this in his own life:

> When we are cursed, we bless (1 Cor. 4:12).

So can it really be that we are meant to join in the Psalms that encourage us to pray *against* our enemies?

A common but unsatisfactory solution

In view of this seeming contradiction, perhaps the most common response has been along the following lines. First it is said, that these sentiments in the Psalms express the honest and entirely understandable feelings of believers under the most terrible pressures, as they experience almost unbelievable pain and utterly unfair treatment. So C. S. Lewis describes them as 'profoundly natural'[16] and Peter Craigie as 'the real and natural reactions to the experience of evil and pain.'[17] Derek Kidner says they 'have the shocking immediacy of a scream, to startle us into feeling something of the desperation which produced them.'[18]

This is undoubtedly true, and is a major reason why those of us who have never experienced such persecution

---

16. Lewis 1961, chapter 2.

17. Craigie 1983:41.

18. Kidner 1972:28.

or ill-treatment for Christ find it so hard to identify with these prayers. As we sit in comfort, sipping our cappuccinos in Islington, we tut-tut at people losing their equanimity in this regrettable way. Our brothers and sisters in the persecuted church, who have seen their fellow-believers beaten, imprisoned, or killed for Christ, have no such difficulty understanding how people can feel like this.

But the most common response continues with a second assertion: although these feelings are natural and understandable, it is said, they are still wrong. C. S. Lewis describes them as 'profoundly wrong' and says that 'we should be wicked if we in any way condoned or approved' these prayers.[19] Peter Craigie says that, 'though the sentiments are in themselves evil, they are part of the life of the soul which is bared before God in worship and prayer'; these words 'are often natural and spontaneous' but they are 'not always pure and good.'[20] Derek Kidner asks the question, 'Can a Christian use these cries for vengeance as his own?' and concludes, 'The short answer must surely be "No".'[21]

My guess is that most of us reading this book will be inclined to agree with this kind of response. But before we relax and think we have solved the problem, we need to face up to a number of reasons why it is unsatisfactory.

Why this approach is unsatisfactory?
We cannot drive a wedge between the OT and the NT
We need first to clear away the common but shallow assertion that the Psalms include the kind of sub-Christian material we expect in the Old Testament, and that we should be New

19. Lewis 1961, chapter 2.
20. Craigie 1983:41.
21. Kidner 1972:32.

Testament people rather than Old Testament people. In one episode of *The West Wing*, President Jed Bartlet defends the Bible against an accusation that the Old Testament is bloodthirsty by saying, 'I'm more of a New Testament man myself.' This kind of thing is typically said by those who know little of the Old Testament, or of the New for that matter. When Paul teaches, 'Do not take revenge, my dear friends, but leave room for God's wrath' in Romans 12, he supports this with quotations from Deuteronomy 32:35 and Proverbs 25:21-22 (Rom. 12:19-20). The Old Testament is his authority for forbidding personal revenge. When Peter writes, 'Do not repay evil with evil or insult with insult' his authority is from Psalm 34 (1 Pet. 3:9-12). David refuses to take revenge on King Saul; instead he says, 'May the LORD judge between you and me. And may the LORD avenge the wrongs you have done to me, but my hand will not touch you' (1 Sam. 24:12). The New Testament follows the Old Testament in consistently opposing personal revenge.

Further, there are striking prayers for cursing in the New Testament. Paul writes, 'If anyone does not love the Lord, let that person be cursed!' On another occasion he says, 'But even if we or an angel from heaven should preach a gospel other than the one we preached to you, let them be under God's curse' (1 Cor. 16:22 and Gal. 1:8). So the Old Testament has no monopoly on praying for God's curse on the wicked. We cannot evade this difficulty in the Psalms by an uninformed Old Testament/New Testament contrast.

These prayers are inseparable from the rest of the Psalms

Next, we need to face up to the fact that these prayers are woven into the Psalter in such a way that it is very difficult to unpick the threads and remove them. They do not appear in just a few difficult Psalms, which might perhaps be set to one side in our praying; they surface again and again, and sometimes at unexpected moments. 'It is impossible to have the Psalter without its references to godless enemies' and the prayers for their destruction.[22] There is no indication within the Psalms themselves that some parts are authorised responses to God (to be echoed by us) while other parts are natural but unauthorised cries of the anguished soul (to be omitted by us).

So we are faced with a decision: either we regard the Psalms – all the Psalms, and all of all the Psalms – as God-given authorised response to shape our prayers, or we treat the Psalms as a resource for our praying, such that we pick the bits that seem inspiring to us. The trouble is that, if we adopt the latter strategy, we have evacuated the Psalms of their authority, and we might as well take any other pious literature as a resource and inspiration for our praying. Those with a low view of scripture may be happy to do this, but not those who hold to its utter trustworthiness and authority. Dietrich Bonhoeffer wrote that we should not 'pick and choose', for 'otherwise we dishonour God by presuming to know better than he what we should pray.'[23]

We cannot simply spiritualise the enemies

So how do we get around the difficulty? Another suggestion is to spiritualise the enemies against whom the Psalmists pray. So Derek Kidner suggests that the Christian 'may of course translate them into affirmations of God's judgement, and into denunciations of "the spiritual hosts

22. Barth 1966:43.
23. quoted in Anderson 1970:62.

of wickedness" which are the real enemy.'[24] But it is not clear that the Bible authorises us to do this; we cannot evade the fact that the enemies in the Psalms are human enemies. They may act under satanic inspiration, but the agents of hostility are flesh and blood, and it is against these historical men and women that the Psalmists pray.

The New Testament quotes some of these prayers with approval

And there is a further point to note. The New Testament, far from quietly omitting these prayers in the Psalms, quotes from them and says they have been answered in the judgment of God on Judas Iscariot (Acts 1:16-20 quotes from Pss. 69 and 109). Indeed, when the Lord Jesus weeps over Jerusalem and declares that, 'They will dash you to the ground, you and the children within your walls' (Luke 19:41-44), He makes an unmistakeable allusion to Psalm 137:9, where a blessing is pronounced on the one who does just this.

Working towards a solution

So, although this is an acute difficulty for us, we must grapple more deeply to see if there is any way in which we can join in these prayers. We will do this in five stages.

These are prayers, not curses

First, we note that these verses and passages in the Psalms are prayers to God. They are not strictly curses. It is usual to speak of the 'imprecatory Psalms' or 'imprecatory' passages in the Psalms (from the Latin *imprecari*, to invoke harm, or curse someone). But this is misleading. One scholar writes, 'it is doubtful whether these Psalms should be described as

---

24. Kidner 1972:32.

"imprecatory" or cursing Psalms.'[25] The reason for this is that a curse is 'aimed directly, without any detour via God, at the one it is meant to hit. A curse is a word of power which the swearer released without recourse to God.'[26] There is a great difference between letting loose a curse against someone, and praying for God to execute His just judgment on them; in the former, it is a battle between me against my enemy; in the latter, it is a plea that God, who knows all things and acts with perfect justice, will bring about that justice.

They are prayers for God to do what He has promised to do, in His covenant

Second, the prayers to God are precisely in line with the covenant promises of God; the Psalmists are praying that God will do what He has already promised to do. They are 'completely unoriginal'. 'David and the Psalmists didn't choose their curses from a warped imagination, but primarily from their reading of the Law of Moses.'[27] Right back at the start of the covenant with Abraham, God promises, 'I will bless those who bless you, and whoever curses you I will curse' (Gen. 12:3). The most appalling curses in the Bible appear not in the prayers of the Psalmists but in the covenant curses of the Law of Moses (Deut. 27,28). God prophesies in Isaiah that on the day of judgment Babylon's 'infants will be dashed to pieces before their eyes' (Isa. 13:16); Jeremiah says that, 'Babylon must fall because of Israel's slain, just as the slain in all the earth

---

25. Anderson 1970:65.

26. Claus Westermann, quoted in Anderson 1970:65.

27. Andrew Saville, Proclamation Trust teaching day, available online at www.proctrust.org.uk

have fallen because of Babylon' (Jer. 51:49). So the prayer
that horrifies us in Psalm 137:9 is directly in line with the
judgment that God has already declared.

So when a psalmist prays for God to curse an enemy
who has been cursing him, he is praying in line with the
revealed covenant will of God. 'It is mine to avenge; I will
repay,' says the Lord (Deut. 32:35, quoted in Rom. 12:19).
To pray for God to do what God has said He will do is
very different from taking the law into our own hands and
seeking to exact revenge upon our enemies.

These prayers are against God's enemies, and assume that the Psalmist's enemies are the same as God's enemies: ultimately this can only be true of Jesus Christ

Third, these prayers are not about personal enemies, but
about those whose hostility is, first and foremost, against
God, and therefore against God's king and God's people.
'Do I not hate those who hate *you*, LORD, and abhor those
who are in rebellion against *you*?' (Ps. 139:21). This raises
another problem: how can I know that my enemies are
necessarily enemies of God? People may dislike or harm
me for all sorts of reasons, and some of their reasons may
be at least partially justified by my own bad behaviour.
Some of my enemies may be God's enemies, and some of
God's enemies may be my enemies. But plenty may not,
and it would be arrogant and unrealistic of me to suppose
that there is a one-to-one correspondence between the
two. The Psalmists are not saying something like this to
God: 'O LORD, you know that your interests and mine
partly coincide, so please come in and fight on my side even
though you only partly agree with me.' No, the Psalmist
is claiming that he loves God so much that his enemies

are precisely God's enemies. If anyone opposes him, it is because he opposes God.

This cannot be true of any random believer; it can only be true of the covenanted leader of the people of God in his official role as King or leader. It finds its fulfilment in the only man in history who has indeed loved God the Father so much that His enemies are precisely (with one-to-one correspondence) God the Father's enemies. This is a hint – perhaps more than a hint – that the only one who can ultimately pray these prayers is Jesus Christ. He is the only one who can pray these prayers from a sinless heart, with no selfish motives of revenge, such as plague our hearts when we are maligned or wronged. And He is the one who will die the death of sinners to redeem from their sins all who will trust in Him. The only man who can be entrusted with the dignity of executing the judgment of God on sinners (Acts 17:31) is the one who dies for sinners. The wrath that will be finally poured out against hardened impenitence is 'the wrath of the Lamb.'[28] He is the one who becomes the curse of the law on behalf of all who will be His (Gal. 3:10-13).

Conversion is a possible way in which these prayers may be answered

Fourth, conversion is sometimes envisaged as an alternative way in which an enemy of God can be changed. There is a sense in which conversion involves the destruction of an enemy of God, in the sense that the enemy is reconciled with God and becomes God's friend. We see a hint of this in Psalm 83.

---

28. I am grateful to John Woodhouse for this observation.

> Cover their faces with shame, LORD,
>   so that they will seek your name.
> May they ever be ashamed and dismayed;
>   may they perish in disgrace... (Ps. 83:16-17)

There is an ambiguity here. Perhaps they will 'seek your name'; but if they don't, then they must 'perish in disgrace.'[29] We are reminded of Abraham Lincoln's question: 'Do I not destroy my enemies when I make them my friends?'[30]

There is a deep theological truth here. All the curses due to a sinner are borne by Jesus Christ if that sinner comes to repentance and faith. When the Psalms pray for God's judgment to fall, those prayers are answered when the judgments fall upon Christ.

These prayers are against hardened sinners

This leads to our fifth observation, that those who fall under final judgment are those in whom there is hardened opposition and final impenitence. In Psalm 35 David says of his enemies,

> They repay me evil for good
>   and leave me like one bereaved.
> Yet when they were ill, I put on sackcloth
>   and humbled myself with fasting. (Ps. 35:12-13)

That is to say, David's response to their suffering was to pray for them. Only when they persisted in completely

---

29. Goldingay 2006-8:582: 'the Psalm looks beyond their mere defeat to this turning to Yhwh. Such turning will indicate that they have seen the error in their aggressive confrontation of Yhwh. So it is for the truth's sake, for Yhwh's sake, that the Psalm looks for this seeking, even if it will also be a blessing for the attackers themselves.'

30. Address to Illinois legislature, January 1837.

ungrounded opposition does David pray for God to act in judgment (see vv. 14-26).

There is such a thing as 'the sin against the Holy Spirit' (Matt. 12:32) or 'a sin that leads to death' (1 John 5:16), a hardening of the heart that will never be reversed, in which a man or woman turns so deeply against God that they will never turn in repentance to seek forgiveness. If they ever did repent and seek forgiveness, they would find it; their very seeking of forgiveness would prove that they had not committed this unpardonable sin.

This is helpful and humbling to us. It reminds us that we cannot know for sure whether or not someone will be finally impenitent. Had we watched Saul of Tarsus ravaging the church (Acts 8:3) we might have been sure that he was one of the enemies against whom we could pray for God's judgment. Perhaps we would have felt the same had we listened to Simon Peter denying Jesus three times. In both cases we would have been wrong. Again, had we watched Judas Iscariot during the ministry of Jesus, we would have seen an insider, a disciple who looked and sounded like a genuine disciple (e.g. John 13:22). Soberingly, we would have been wrong. It is not for us to know for sure who will be saved in the end.

Can we attach names to these prayers?

This raises the question of whether we can, as it were, attach names to these prayers. How can we know if a particular persecutor, for example, is a hardened enemy (a Judas Iscariot) or a future trophy of grace (a Saul of Tarsus)? The answer is that we can't know. But this may not be a barrier to praying for God's restraining and just judgment on a particular persecutor. Perhaps the early church prayed for

God to act in judgment on Saul of Tarsus. What if they did? A case can be made that when Saul was converted their prayers were answered beyond their wildest dreams. They would come to know that the judgment of God had indeed been visited – but with the sins of Saul falling upon Jesus Christ. The persecutor had been sternly rebuked and repented deeply. And the glory of God – the deepest burden of their praying – would be lifted high. Their response would be awe and wonder at the majestic wisdom of God in answering their prayers more deeply than they had asked. Someone has pointed out that, when Simon Peter was imprisoned (Acts 12), the church prayed for his release, rather than for the conversion of everyone in the prison system! To call for God to answer in ways we can envisage Him doing does not prevent Him answering yet more deeply and richly, with conversions rather than destruction.

Praying these prayers in Christ
Before considering one of the strongest of these Psalms as a worked example, let me outline what I think is the most coherent and biblical way forward.

First, we hear these prayers as fulfilled in the prayers of Jesus Christ. It is true that Jesus prayed for those who crucified Him; but He did so because 'they know not what they do.' There was something about them that did not necessarily indicate a hardened heart. And yet, even more deeply than this, surely He prayed for His Father's will to be done on earth as it is done in heaven; this cannot happen while rebels patrol the earth.

Second, with very great caution and humility, we need to learn to join in Jesus' choir when He sings these prayers. We need to understand that the judgment of God on the finally hardened and impenitent is a necessary and good part of the gospel. It is necessary because it is the essential precondition for the new heavens and new earth to be a pure and holy place. It is good because it will resound to the glory of God. When 'Babylon' – a symbol for the whole anti-God system of the world – falls in Revelation 18 and 19, the people of God do not weep; they sing hallelujahs with great joy. It is this for which they have longed and they grasp that God is glorified in it.

Worked Example: Psalm 109

I take as an example Psalm 109, one of the strongest of the imprecatory Psalms, to explore how we might both teach and pray this Psalm in Christ. The Psalm divides naturally into three unequal parts. First, David tells us the crisis that provokes the prayer (1-5); then he prays against his accusers (6-20); and finally he prays for himself (21-29) before a concluding affirmation of praise (30-31).

A prayer in a crisis (1-5)

> For the director of music. Of David. A Psalm.

> [1] My God, whom I praise,
>   do not remain silent,
> [2] for people who are wicked and deceitful
>   have opened their mouths against me;
>   they have spoken against me with lying tongues.
> [3] With words of hatred they surround me;
>   they attack me without cause.
> [4] In return for my friendship they accuse me,
>   but I am a man of prayer. (that is, David has prayed
>   for them, cf. Psalm 35:13)
> [5] They repay me evil for good,
>   and hatred for my friendship.

The Psalm begins with praise (1 'My God, whom I praise…');
it will end with praise (30 '…I will greatly extol the LORD…I
will praise him…'). The bookending of the Psalm with praise
reminds us that, whatever else we do with the Psalm, above
all it should issue in heartfelt praise. We are going to learn
something profoundly good and praiseworthy about God.

But after the initial praise, verses 1-5 give us an insight
into the crisis that has prompted David to pray. There are
noisy accusations ('opened their mouths…spoken…words
of hatred…accuse me…'), but – to David's dismay – a silent
God (1b 'do not remain silent'). The issue is set as one of
words. Words are spoken against the King; the King pleads
with God to speak words in his vindication.

These enemies are wicked in character (2a 'wicked'),
malicious in motivation (3 'words of hatred'), deceitful in their
methods (2 'deceitful…lying tongues'), unjustified in their
hostility (3 'without cause'; 4 'In return for my friendship';
5 'evil for good'), and the way in which they attack David
is precisely by accusation (4 'they accuse me'). Further, they
are not enemies from afar; they were David's friends (4 'In
return for my friendship…'). Just as in Psalm 35:13 David
says he has grieved with them when they grieved, so here he
has done them nothing but good. And yet they accuse him.

In David's life we might think of King Saul in the early
years, or Doeg the Edomite, who betrays David to Saul
(1 Sam. 21, 22 – see 22:9). Later on, during Absalom's
rebellion, Ahithophel, David's trusted counsellor, goes over
to the side of the rebellion (2 Sam. 15:12-31).

Prayer against his accusers (6-20)
Most of the prayer is against one particular enemy, pre-
sumably the leader of the hostile band. In verse 20 this

is broadened to 'my accusers' in the plural. As we hear this prayer, let us note five features that help us to see the rightness of it.

Note that it is a prayer (6-8)
First – and this is so obvious it is easy to miss – David is praying a prayer. He is not letting loose a curse, but praying for God to act.

> [6] Appoint someone evil to oppose my enemy;
>   let an accuser stand at his right hand.

An 'accuser' (literally 'a satan') is exactly what this man has been against David (4). To stand 'at the right hand' is a law court image: this is where the witness stands, either for the prosecution or for the defence. We meet it again in verse 31, where the LORD 'stands at the right hand of the needy' to vindicate them. The core issue is the condemnation or the vindication of God's King. David prays that this accuser will be condemned because only by the accusation being removed can he, the King, be vindicated. It is one or the other.

> [7] When he is tried, let him be found guilty,
>   and may his prayers condemn him.

Again, this is law court language. This accuser is a wicked man; if his prayers were to be heard, there would be no justice in the universe. It is important that his prayers lead to his condemnation, because they are not true prayers.

> [8] May his days be few;
>   may another take his place of leadership.

It is all prayer language: 'Appoint…let…let…may…may… may…'

Note the seriousness of the issue (8)
This man is not doing David a personal wrong. David is the anointed King and this man is in a 'place of leadership'. He is committing treason, which is the most serious wrongdoing imaginable, precisely because it threatens the fabric of society by cutting to the heart of the leadership of the people. The King is 'the LORD's anointed,' the one 'under (whose) shadow' they thought they would live in safety (cf. Lam. 4:20). To threaten the King is to threaten everyone.

We might think of Vidkun Quisling, one time Norwegian Minister of Defence, who became the willing head of the puppet government of Norway when the Nazis invaded in 1940. Quisling's crime of treason was so serious that he was executed in 1945. Or Kim Philby, Head of British Counter-Intelligence during the Cold War years, but actually spying for the Soviet Union, passing on information that sent countless British and American operatives to their deaths over a period of twenty years. He deserved to die.

So the crime about which David prays is not a personal slight or wrong; it is high treason against God's anointed King.

Note the significance of familial solidarity (9-15)
The next section is perhaps what troubles us most, for in it David prays, not only against this traitor, but against his family.

> 9 May his children be fatherless
> and his wife a widow.
> 10 May his children be wandering beggars;
> may they be driven from their ruined homes.
> 11 May a creditor seize all he has;
> may strangers plunder the fruits of his labour.

¹² May no one extend kindness to him
     or take pity on his fatherless children.
¹³ May his descendants be cut off,
     their names blotted out from the next generation.
¹⁴ May the iniquity of his fathers be remembered before
     the LORD;
     may the sin of his mother never be blotted out.
¹⁵ May their sins always remain before the LORD,
     that he may blot out their name from the earth.

We can understand verse 9, for it is the necessary conse-
quence of this traitor being executed; by definition, his
children will become fatherless and his wife a widow. But is
it necessary for David to pray with such vehemence against
the children and subsequent generations of this man's
family? We tend to think David is being vindictive. But we
need to consider this: men and women are not free-floating
individuals, as we so often think of ourselves in western
cultures. On the contrary, we are creatures shaped by our
families and our culture. Our default convictions are the
background beliefs and behaviour of our culture and family.
Unless something wonderful happens to break us out of
these corporate solidarities, we will behave as our fathers
did. The Amalekites hated the people of God at the time of
the Exodus (Exod. 17:8-16). Their descendant Agag, King
of Amalek, fought against the people of God in the time of
King Saul half a millennium later (1 Sam. 15). And, half
a millennium after that, Haman the Agagite, sharing that
corporate solidarity, hated the people of God (Esther 3).

It is possible – wonderfully possible – that someone
may repent and leave the 'generation' in which they were
born and nurtured (cf. Acts 2:40 'Save yourselves from this
corrupt generation'), as Ruth the Moabitess so wonderfully

did (Ruth 1:16-17). But in so doing she ceased in her heart to be a true Moabite and was grafted in to Israel. King David prays against the family of this traitor because the normal and natural expectation is that his family will share his nature. And as long as they do, the earth will never be a safe place until that family are 'blotted out…from the earth' (15). So there is a reason and a necessary logic in what David here prays.

Note the justice in what David prays (16-19)

> [16] For he never thought of doing a kindness,
>   but hounded to death the poor
>   and the needy and the broken-hearted.
> [17] He loved to pronounce a curse –
>   may it come back on him.
>   He found no pleasure in blessing –
>   may it be far from him.
> [18] He wore cursing as his garment;
>   it entered into his body like water,
>   into his bones like oil.
> [19] May it be like a cloak wrapped about him,
>   like a belt tied for ever round him.

The punishment for which David prays precisely fits the crime this man has committed. Notice how this man is not at root a good man who happens to have slipped up with this one act of betrayal. He loved to pronounce a curse on others and found no pleasure in blessing others (17); so much so that 'he wore cursing as his garment,' it became like his clothing; and, more than that, 'it entered into his body like water, into his bones (his inner being) like oil' (18). Cursing became an integral and inseparable part of his character. It was not just that he issued a curse; he became a curse, and therefore accursed. The judgment for which

David prays precisely accords with the accursed character of this terrible traitor.

Note how David prays according to the will of God (20)

> [20] May this be the LORD's payment to my accusers,
> to those who speak evil of me.

The LORD had promised Abraham that those who cursed his people, God would curse (Gen. 12:3). These people – this traitor and his band – spoke evil of David. And in so doing they sealed their own fate and placed themselves under the covenant curse of God. David prays that God will do what God has committed Himself to do.

Prayer for himself, the anointed King (21-29)

In the final main section, David prays for himself. There is a pitiful intensity about his petitions. Here we may note a sixth feature of David's prayer, to add to the five noted in the last section.

Note David's godly motivation, for the honour of the LORD

> [21] But you, Sovereign LORD,
> help me for your name's sake;
> out of the goodness of your love, deliver me.

David prays all that he prays 'for your name's sake'. That is to say, he does not pray it for his own sake, but so that the reputation and honour of God will be upheld. People need to know that there is a faithful covenant God who keeps His promises to His anointed King. And the only way they can know is if this treachery does not go unpunished. It would be an outrage to the honour of God for this to happen. This is the heartbeat of David's prayer.

²² For I am poor and needy,
>   and my heart is wounded within me.

²³ I fade away like an evening shadow;
>   I am shaken off like a locust.

²⁴ My knees give way from fasting;
>   my body is thin and gaunt.

²⁵ I am an object of scorn to my accusers;
>   when they see me, they shake their heads.

²⁶ Help me, LORD my God;
>   save me according to your unfailing love
>   (covenant love).

²⁷ Let them know that it is your hand,
>   that you, LORD, have done it.

²⁸ While they curse, may you bless (that is, bless your
>   anointed King and his people);
>   may those who attack me be put to shame,
>   but may your servant rejoice.

²⁹ May my accusers be clothed with disgrace
>   and wrapped in shame as in a cloak.

The issue is still the condemnation or the vindication of God's King. The most terrible thing about these enemies is that they are 'accusers' (25, 29). The whole motivation and reason for David's prayer is that the honour of God will be upheld as He vindicates the anointed King He has promised to vindicate.

Concluding praise (30-31)

³⁰ With my mouth I will greatly extol the LORD;
>   in the great throng of worshippers I will
>   praise him.

³¹ For he stands at the right hand of the needy,
>   to save their lives from those who would
>   condemn them.

The big reason that undergirds David's praise ('for' – v. 31) is that 'he stands at the right hand of the needy, to save their lives from those who would condemn them'. In the law court the anointed King and the believing people are threatened with condemnation. At their right hand stand false witnesses accusing them, calling for their condemnation. But, gloriously, at their right hand stands one who saves their lives, who contradicts the accusations, and speaks the authoritative voice of justification and vindication.

Who can pray this prayer?

At first reading, this is a very difficult prayer. It looks superficially like being told to kneel down piously at one's bedside and pray like this:

> Dear God, my loving heavenly Father, I want to pray about so-and-so (my boss, my awkward neighbour, my difficult family member). You know how difficult he has been and what problems he is causing me. So please may he die – and pretty soon. May his children become wandering beggars. May no-one take pity on them, so the whole wider family dies out. Will you do that for me, dear God? Thank you, loving heavenly Father. In Jesus' name, Amen.

If we think that is what this Psalm is inviting us to pray, we are right to refuse! But it is not. Here is a man, betrayal of whom threatens the government of the world, a man so utterly righteous that betrayal of Him is 100 per cent unjustified, a man who, when falsely accused, entrusts Himself in prayer to the God who judges justly and refuses to take personal revenge, a man who prays out of absolutely pure motives, simply for the honour of God. Above all, who so loves sinners that He bears the curse for all who will trust in Him. This is the voice – finally – of Jesus the Anointed King, who alone can lead the people of God in such dangerous but necessary prayers.

The New Testament confirms that this is – in the end – a prayer of Jesus. Satan – the accuser – entered into the heart of Judas Iscariot (John 13:27). This prayer is the prayer of the Son of God against His treacherous accuser and betrayer. Although Jesus prayed for those who crucified Him (Luke 23:34), it is a sobering thought that, so far as we know, He never prayed for Judas. He loved him; He gave him every opportunity to repent; and yet somehow He knew that Judas' treachery had to be. And when it came to the moment, Jesus simply told him to go (John 13:27). He spoke of him, no doubt with tears in His eyes, as the one doomed to destruction (John 17:12). There is such a thing as hardened evil, such that a man will never repent. Elsewhere, Jesus calls it the blasphemy against the Holy Spirit (Mark 3:28-29). John calls it 'sin that leads to death' (1 John 5:16-17). We cannot tell who is committing this unpardonable sin. Some who are terribly deep in sin will wonderfully repent, as Saul of Tarsus did. Others who appear to be at the heart of the apostolic band, like Judas Iscariot, will turn out to be in the grip of evil. But for this hardness, it is right to pray for the justice of God to take its course.

Peter quotes from verse 8 in Acts 1:20 (as well as from another imprecatory Psalm, Ps. 69): 'May another take his place of leadership.' This Psalm finds its fulfilment as the righteous prayer of God's anointed Messiah as He prays for final vindication, a vindication that comes when His accuser is condemned and He Himself is raised from the dead. But it continues to have application, as the church of

Christ pray that the voice of resolute impenitent hostility, the heirs and successors of Judas and the continuing mouthpieces of Satan, be stopped and the children of God finally vindicated, as we trust we shall be.

In this age we pray for those who persecute us (Matt. 5:44); we bless our enemies and do not curse them (Rom. 12:14). We do not know which of our enemies will be wonderfully converted, and we pray that they will. But we also pray, joining with Jesus our Head in this Psalm, that in the end the finally impenitent voices of hostility will be silenced and the righteous vindicated. With great care, and only in Christ, we too may join in this Psalm. David is a type, so that,

> everything that is expressed in this Psalm must properly
> be applied to Christ, the Head of the Church, and to all
> the faithful inasmuch as they are his members; so that
> when unjustly treated and tormented by their enemies,
> they may apply to God to help, to whom vengeance
> belongs.[31]

---

31. Calvin 1993, Vol.VI, p. 268.

Part Three:

INTEGRATING THE PSALMS INTO THE BIBLE STORY

All the major themes of Old Testament history and theology may be heard and savoured in the Psalms. Indeed, those who soak themselves in the Psalms discover – as a happy side-effect – that they develop a wide and deep appreciation of the Old Testament as a whole. The converse is also true: to enjoy the richness of the Psalms needs a commitment to growing a deep knowledge of the Old Testament.'[1]

The purpose of this part of our handbook is to give some tools for detecting and interpreting some of the main historical motifs in the Psalms as they relate to six key points in the Bible story: Creation, Abraham, the Exodus, Sinai, Zion, and the Exile. We also consider the twin motifs of lament and praise that run right through the Psalter.

---

1. 'The Book of Psalms is a virtual compendium of themes and topics found in the rest of the Old Testament…The Psalms in their common and constant use constitute one of the most important ways in which the Old Testament is known in the church.' Mays 1994:1f.

9. Creation in the Psalms

How do the Psalms portray the world in which we live? The short answer is that it is God's Creation. But what do we mean by this? A few Psalms contain concentrated Creation language: Psalms 8, 19, 104, and 148 are the most significant. But Creation language is woven into many Psalms.

The purpose of this chapter is to help you notice and understand Creation language in the Psalms. I will do this under seven headings.

God is transcendent over all Creation and yet immanent in it

First, listen in the Psalms for the underlying confidence that God is the eternal Creator of the whole universe. He made it all.

God is before, beyond, and outside of time. 'Before the mountains were born' – a picture of the oldest part of Creation – 'or you brought forth the whole world, from everlasting to everlasting you are God' (Ps. 90:2). In the Apostles Creed we affirm that God is 'the Maker of heaven and earth.' This comes from the Psalms: Psalms 115:15, 121:2, 124:8, 134:3. The expression 'heaven and earth' (technically a merism) encompasses the high things and the low things and everything in between (as in Gen. 1:1). There is no part, no facet, no feature, no corner of the universe that has not been created by God, visible and invisible, large and small, animate and inanimate, material and immaterial.

Or, to put this same truth in another way, there is no god but the God of the Bible. All other spirits or so-called gods are part of the universe. They have no objective real existence outside of, or independent from, the universe; if the universe ceased to exist, they would cease to exist. But the Creator God is self-existent. 'If I were hungry I would not tell you, for the world is mine and all that is in it' (Ps. 50:12). 'Among the gods there is none like you, Lord... you alone are God' (Ps. 86:8-10).

It follows that the God of the Bible is utterly sovereign over the whole universe. 'The Lord reigns...' (e.g. Ps. 99:1). He brought the universe into existence by His command, His word, and His Spirit (Pss. 33:6, 148:5-6). He rules the universe by His decree. All of it. Psalm 104 expresses this transcendence in vivid poetic terms: 'he stretches out the heavens like a tent and lays the beams of his upper chambers on their waters' (Ps. 104:2-3). The sky is like a ceiling (the firmament) above which are waters, store-chambers for rain, hail, and snow. Above these waters God sets up His dwelling-place, His 'heavens' (not here the sky, but the dwelling-place of God above the sky). He does it with the ease with which an experienced nomad or camper might set up a tent. And He does it *above* the waters. This matters. Human existence, and indeed the existence of supernatural spiritual beings, lies between the waters beneath and the waters above the firmament. This is why the demons may be said to live in 'the air' (Eph. 2:2) but not in the highest heaven. All such existence, human or spiritual, is under threat from the waters. God alone sets up His dwelling above the waters. He is 'enthroned over the flood' (Ps. 29:10), for 'he builds his lofty palace in the heavens' (Amos 9:6). His government cannot be threatened by chaos or evil, for He is transcendent. Creation depends upon Him, not He upon it.

But although the Lord dwells above the waters (He is transcendent), nevertheless He is active within Creation (immanent). The created stuff of the universe is His instrument to work His will. 'He makes the clouds his chariot and rides on the wings of the wind.' He flies around Creation on a chariot-throne. 'He makes winds his messengers, flames of fire (lightning) his servants' (Ps. 104:3-4). What we see, detect, and experience, are all the servants and instruments with which, or with whom, God works His will. God Himself is invisible, but He uses the visible, detectable stuff of the universe to carry out His purposes. 'Lightning and hail, snow and clouds, stormy winds…do his bidding' (Ps. 148-8). Every cause, each firing of a neural pathway, this weather phenomenon and that social trend, each and every one is God's instrument to work His will.

We live in a world under the shadow of death[2]
Having affirmed this, the Psalms portray for us vividly a world under threat. As in the book of Job, the poetic description of the world paints a picture of solid ground surrounded by terrifying waters. On the solid ground you know where you stand; you can live and survive there. But there are waters below and around you; and there are waters above the firmament (a kind of ceiling) of the sky. Any or all of these waters threaten to engulf the habitable earth and drown us all. These waters have raging waves. They 'roar and foam' making the mountains 'quake with their surging' (Ps. 46:2-3). At any moment deep waters may call to deep waters 'in the roar of your waterfalls' and then 'all your waves and breakers' will sweep 'over me' (Ps. 42:7).

In these waters, sometimes called 'the deep' are the entrances to Sheol, where the dead go. The torrents of water are therefore not merely a threatening material phenomenon;

---

2. Barth 1966:49-55 and Anderson 1970:89f .

they are the instruments of death itself. Death in the Psalms is not simply an event that happens on the last day of our lives. Death is an enemy, like a many-headed monster with tentacles. 'The cords (or tentacles) of death entangled me; the torrents of destruction overwhelmed me. The cords of the grave coiled around me; the snares of death confronted me' (Ps. 18:4-5). It is rather like the horrifying 'Watcher in the Water' with its tentacles threatening the Fellowship of the Ring by the Westgate to the Mines of Moria in *The Lord of the Rings*.

Death has a 'realm' or kingdom (e.g. Pss. 30:3; 49:15; 86:13); it is like an imperialistic aggressor, seeking to augment his territory by conquest over the living. Always he is attacking, pushing, pressing home his advantage, never resting, never content. Every time you or I get a cold, the tentacles of death reach out to pull us down to Sheol. When we feel tired, are aware of getting older and weaker, when we feel the pull of some addictive and destructive behaviour or the allure of sin, when we are imprisoned or restricted, when anything happens that reduces our overall peace and wellbeing, the tentacles of death coil themselves around us to drag us down to the place of the dead. With this vivid imagery, the Psalms convey to us something of the visceral horror we ought to feel living in a world under the shadow of death. In the Psalms, it is not that we are alive now, but in danger of dying later; rather we are, here and now, walking in the shadow of death. To pray, as the Psalmists do, for God to 'deliver them from death' is not to pray that this life will be allowed to continue without death intervening as an unwelcome interruption; it is to call upon God to rescue us from this so-called life, which in reality is always shadowed by death.

What is more, the deep sea is the home of a terrible sea monster, sometimes called Leviathan (Pss. 74:14, 104:26), sometimes Rahab (Ps. 89:10). Who or what is this monster? At one level, it is just a very big sea creature, something like a whale, perhaps. But elsewhere in the Old Testament (to say nothing of Ancient Near Eastern stories), Leviathan is a monster, 'a gliding serpent…a coiling serpent…the monster of the sea' (Isa. 27:1). The overtones of the name 'Leviathan' are dark, dangerous and satanic. He is the embodiment of evil, Satan himself. He is the serpent of Genesis 3, the monster of Job 41, Satan himself (Rev. 12:9). He is a real and terrifying creature with the power of death (Heb. 2:14). And yet, with deep irony, Psalm 104 describes him as nothing more than a creature made by God 'to frolic' in the sea (Ps. 104:26)! He is rather like a swimming teddy bear, God's pet, who plays around in the sea, which God has made as his playpen! Leviathan is like a bumptious toddler, whom a careful parent has boxed in with a playpen so that he cannot wreak havoc elsewhere. He has no autonomy, no existence, no power independent of the Creator.

We live in a world that is stable and ordered

It follows that, in spite of the reality and terror of the waters and the shadow of death, the Psalms portray this world as finally a safe place, because of our Sovereign Creator. God has made the Creation a place of order. Not just material order, without which science would not be possible, but moral order. He made the world 'in wisdom' (Ps. 104:24), 'by understanding' (Ps. 136:5). The words 'wisdom' and 'understanding' are shorthands for the Order of Creation, the moral and material ordering that is given to Creation as a non-negotiable and as a gift. Wisdom or understanding is the architecture or blueprint of the world, the underlying laws of order.[3]

What is more, God has not simply begun Creation with order; He guarantees the survival of that order, and the final restoration of that order. The key words in most English translations of the Psalms are 'founded' and 'established'. Psalm 93 describes the attack of the seas on the earth: 'The seas have lifted up, LORD, the seas have lifted up their voice; the seas have lifted up their pounding waves.' And yet, 'Mightier than the thunder of the great waters, mightier than the breakers of the sea – the LORD on high is mighty.' And therefore, because 'the LORD reigns,' it follows that, 'the world is *established*, firm and secure.' God is like a reliable builder, whose structure survives all attacks upon it. Psalm 24 begins by affirming that 'the earth is the LORD's, and everything in it, the world, and all who live in it; for he *founded* it on the seas and *established* it on the waters' (Ps. 24:1-2).

Psalm 104:5-9 expound this stability with reference to what God did with the waters in the Creation. The Psalmist affirms, 'He set the earth on its foundations; it can never be moved.' Verses 6-9 tell us why. At the beginning of Creation the 'watery depths' (the 'Deep' with all its connotations of danger) 'covered' the whole earth like 'a garment'. Even 'above the mountains' these Creation waters stood. 'Darkness was over the surface of the deep' (Gen. 1:2). As Milton put it,

> Over all the face of the earth
> Main ocean flowed[4]

---

3. O'Donovan 1994 and cf.Ash 2003, chapter 4.

4. John Milton, *Paradise Lost* 8.278, quoted in Wilcock.

And then God speaks, or rather He shouts a cry of command and rebuke: 'Go! Scram!' He tells the waters in no uncertain terms to flee, and they do – pouring helter-skelter over the mountains, down into the valleys and 'to the place you assigned for them,' that is to say, the oceans. And then (v. 9) God set in place the coastline as a boundary 'they cannot cross' so that 'never again will they cover the earth.' The earth is like a stable island surrounded by threatening waters, but safe because God has made it so. It is *terra firma*, 'founded…on the seas' (Ps. 24:2).

Proverbs 8 tells the story in similar terms:

> when he gave the sea its *boundary*
> so that the waters would not overstep his command,
> and when he marked out the *foundations* of the earth.
>   (Prov. 8:29)

The times when the boundaries are breached, literally by a destructive tsunami, metaphorically by a terrorist attack, an accident, an illness, a sudden death, do not contradict this truth. On the contrary, they bring home to us precisely that, 'the earth would be swallowed up every moment were it not preserved by the secret power of God.'[5] The Genesis flood teaches exactly the same truth.

This theme of the finally guaranteed stability of the world ultimately trumps the motif of threat in the Psalms (e.g. Pss. 78:69, 102:25, 104:5, 148:6). The Creator who established moral order in the world will one day re-establish that order: 'Let all creation rejoice before the Lord, for he comes, he comes to judge the earth. He will judge the world in righteousness and the peoples in his faithfulness' (Ps. 96:13).

---

5. Calvin.

We live in a world for which God generously provides
The fourth Creation motif to watch for in the Psalms is Providence, God's gracious and generous provision for all living creatures.

One of the paradoxical shifts to watch for in the Psalms is how water can be transformed from threat to life-giving provision. This happens in Psalm 104 when verses 5-9 continue in verses 10-18. Here are two other examples. Psalm 135 affirms that, 'The Lord does whatever pleases him, in the heavens and on the earth' and specifically 'in the seas and all their depths'; so the deep sea, with all its threat, is a part of God's purposeful ordering of Creation. We begin to see how in the next verse: 'He makes clouds rise from the ends of the earth; he sends lightning with the rain and brings out the wind from his storehouses' (Ps. 135:6-7). Without the sea there would be no clouds; without the clouds, we would have no rain. Psalm 147 develops this: 'He covers the sky with clouds; he supplies the earth with rain and makes grass grow on the hills. He provides food for the cattle...' (Ps. 147:8-9). The terrifying picture of waters roaring and foaming that begins Psalm 46 is immediately followed by the life-giving, 'There is a *river* whose streams make glad the city of God' (Ps. 46:1-4). While studying Psalm 104, my wife and I enjoyed a few days' holiday on the west of Scotland. It is a place of almost intoxicating beauty – the lochs, the light in summer, the mountains, the heather. It makes us glad. It was meant to. 'All reality is a sign of the goodness and kindness of the Creator.'[6]

In his lovely poem *Spring*, Gerard Manley-Hopkins writes,

---

6. Jörg Jeremias, quoted in Goldingay 2006-8:182.

Nothing is so beautiful as Spring
>   When weeds, in wheels, shoot long and lovely and
>   lush;
>   Thrush's eggs look little low heavens, and thrush
> Through the echoing timber does so rinse and wring
> The ear, it strikes like lightnings to hear him sing;
>   The glassy peartree leaves and blooms, they brush
>   The descending blue; that blue is all in a rush
> With richness; the racing lambs too have fair their fling.

And then he asks,

>   What is all this juice and all this joy?
>   A strain of the earth's sweet being in the beginning
>   In Eden garden.[7]

A corollary of God's providence is our utter dependence upon Him. Psalm 104 develops this in verses 27-30. When God 'opens his hand' we are 'satisfied with good things,' but when He 'hides his face' we are 'terrified…die and return to the dust.'

We live in a world that we are intended to govern

The fifth theme I want to highlight is the unique dignity and responsibility of human beings. We find this, perhaps most famously, in Psalm 8, with its awe-struck reflection on the task given in Genesis 1 to God's image-bearer. In Psalm 139 there is a famous and beloved description of God's intimate care for a human being, knit together in the mother's womb, all their days written in God's book before one of them came to be, a creature with a unique dignity and special place in the Created Order. This theme overflows into what the Psalms say about God's King,

---

7. Gerard Manley Hopkins, *Spring*, 1918.

who is to be a Second Adam to bring God's blessing to the whole world. Psalm 72 is a prayer that the King will come who will fulfil this noble calling.

The flip side of this is where the Psalms condemn powerful men for their abuse of their position. Psalm 82 describes powerful human beings as 'gods.' As a result of their dark behaviour 'all the foundations of the earth are shaken.' Their abuse of power threatens justice; the whole moral order is attacked when human beings behave like this.

So, both positively (the King and Ps. 8) and negatively (Ps. 82) watch for the great significance of human beings as God's image-bearers.

We live in a world that reveals the godness of God
The Psalms describe Creation in terms of a revelation of the 'glory' of God. 'Glory' is the outwardly visible and sensible shining of God's inward being. 'The heavens declare the glory of God; the skies proclaim the work of his hands' (Ps. 19:1). There is a revelation of the godness of God in the Created Order although, as we shall see, it is a partial revelation, sufficient to condemn our idolatry but not sufficient to lead us to salvation (cf. Rom. 1:20).

Psalm 104 proclaims that God is 'clothed with splendour and majesty,' or – for this is another way of saying the same thing – that he 'wraps himself in light as with a garment' (Ps. 104:1-2). Light is the visible, splendid revelation of the majesty of the invisible God. Light stands here as short-hand for the whole Created Order, of which it was the first part. It is both the visible phenomenon that makes us know that God is present, and – at the same time – the impenetrable brightness that conceals His nature: 'Light is a cloak which reveals God's majesty and conceals the divine nature'[8] just as in Ezekiel's vision, the radiant light at the heart of the chariot-throne of God revealed God's presence while concealing His inner nature (Ezek. 1).

When God said, 'Let there be light,' He clothed Himself in a visible 'robe of imperial majesty.'[9] Whereas an invisibility cloak (whether in H. G. Wells' *The Invisible Man* or in Harry Potter) makes a visible person become invisible, the Created Order is like a 'visibility cloak' worn by the invisible God to make something of His presence visible.

The parallel between the Lord wrapping Himself in light and the Lord clothing Himself in splendour and majesty suggests that the Universe is the visible splendour and majesty of the invisible God. Creation 'declares the glory of God' (cf. Ps. 19:1). We cannot see God, but 'must cast our eyes upon the very beautiful fabric of the world in which he wishes to be seen by us' (Calvin). 'The world is charged with the grandeur of God. It will flame out like shining from shook foil.'[10]

We ought to respond by praising our Creator

When the Psalms summon us to praise God for His 'mighty works' or His 'wonders' their voices call us to the only proper response of creatures to the Creator. Perhaps Psalm 148 does this more fully than any other, with its catalogue of hearers, from the heavens above to all the creatures in the earth beneath. The heavenly beings are to praise the Lord, 'for at his command they were created, and he established them for ever and ever' (vv. 5-6); earthly creatures are to praise His name, 'for his name alone is

---

8. Schaefer 2001:257.

9. Kirkpatrick.

10. Gerard Manley Hopkins, *God's Grandeur*, 1877.

exalted; his splendour is above the earth and the heavens'
(v. 13). When praying the Psalms, do not skim over this
call; it is fundamental to true humanness, that we praise
the God who has given us every breath of life.

What does it mean to pray Creation themes in the Psalms 'in Christ'?

Some say that because Jesus is God, Jesus is therefore the
Creator, and when we praise the Creator we praise Jesus. In
our teaching, Jesus becomes little more than an arbitrary
'add on' to God. We need to be more careful. We need,
first, to take seriously the full humanity of Jesus Christ.
Jesus is not God, if by that we mean that 'God is Jesus,' and
therefore 'God' and 'Jesus' are interchangeable. Jesus is the
Son of God, or God the Son; He is God incarnate, fully
man and fully God.

Further, in His earthly life, Jesus did not speak of Himself as the Creator. He did actions that showed the Creator's
authority, but He did not speak of Himself as the Creator.
Indeed, He addressed His Father as 'Lord of heaven and
earth' (Matt. 11:25), which is a title for the Creator God.
He 'offered up prayers and petitions with fervent cries and
tears to the one who could save him from death' (Heb. 5:7),
that is to say, the Creator and giver of life. What is more,
the New Testament does not call Jesus 'the Creator'; it
speaks of Him consistently as the agent *through whom* the
world was made (John 1:3, 1 Cor. 8:6, Heb. 1:2); God the
Father is the Creator.

So it is entirely appropriate, when the Psalms proclaim the praises of the Creator, to hear Jesus Christ our
Lord leading His church in those praises. But it is not only
appropriate; it is necessary. After a magnificent celebration

of Creation Psalm 104 ends with three parallel prayers
(vv. 31-35). In verse 31 the Psalmist prays that God's glory
(that is, the Created Order) may endure for ever; this it will
do only if the Lord rejoices in His works. For, if they do
not please Him, they will not endure (see v. 32). Then in
verses 33-34, he prays that he himself will rejoice, not in
the Created Order, but in the Lord who made it. Finally,
in verse 35, he prays that sinners will vanish from the
earth, because it is sinners who spoil the world and make it
displeasing to God. For the world to endure, it must please
its Creator; it will only do that when sinners are removed.
This gives us a deep problem; for, if we pray it, we pray for
our own exclusion. Only one man so loves God the Father
that He can pray with a pure heart to delight in the Father,
that the world will please the Father, and that sinners will
be removed. Only Jesus Christ can ultimately pray this
Psalm; and we can pray it only in Him.

10. Abraham in the Psalms

Abraham hardly gets a mention in the Psalms. Only two
of the Psalms include his name (Pss. 47 and 105). So this
may seem a strange chapter to include! But let's think more
deeply. Abraham does not have to be named for Abraham
to be in the Psalmists' minds and on their hearts.

The core conviction underlying the remembering of Abraham is that God keeps His promises. Back in Genesis 12 the
LORD made a promise to Abraham:

> Go from your country, your people and your father's
>   household to the land I will show you.
>
> I will make you into a great nation,
>   and I will bless you;

> I will make your name great,
>> and you will be a blessing.
>
> I will bless those who bless you,
>> and whoever curses you I will curse;
> and all peoples (or 'families') on earth
>> will be blessed through you. (Gen. 12:1-3)

As Genesis develops, this promise is reiterated and expanded to Abraham in Genesis 15, called a covenant in Genesis 17, repeated in many places, and then reapplied to Isaac and to Jacob. Three elements of this covenant are significant in the Psalms: the land, the curse, and worldwide blessing.

The land

When 'the land' is mentioned in the Psalms it generally refers to the Promised Land, that is to say, the land promised first to Abraham in Genesis 12. This land is also called an 'inheritance'. So when the Psalms speak of the land or the inheritance, Abraham is there in the deep background.

The curse

God promises to curse those who curse Abraham and his seed. We have seen in chapter 8 that the prayers in the Psalms for God to curse His enemies have their roots in this promise God has made to Abraham. To curse Abraham's seed is to be the enemy of the God who has chosen and blessed Abraham, and therefore to deserve punishment. God has chosen to set His love on Abraham and his seed, and therefore the proper response of every human being is to want to be identified with Abraham and his seed, since this is the locus in which we experience God's blessing. Deliberately not to do this, but to set oneself against these people, has its roots in the heart's hostility towards God.

Worldwide blessing

God promises Abraham that he will become a great nation, so great that the whole world will be blessed through his seed. It becomes clear that this blessing will come from being governed by Abraham's seed: nations and kings will come from him to rule the world (Gen. 17:6).

The Abraham connection is explicit in Psalm 47. Here the people of God summon 'all you nations' to 'shout to God with cries of joy' (v. 1) because the LORD is 'the great King over all the earth' (v. 2 and v. 7), 'nations' are 'subdued' under the people of God (v. 3), we are given our 'inheritance' (v. 4, that is the Promised Land) and 'God reigns over the nations' (v. 8). The climax of the Psalm rejoices that,

> The nobles of the nations assemble
> > as the people of the God of Abraham,
> for the kings of the earth belong to God;
> > he is greatly exalted. (v. 9)

Repeatedly, the King in David's line is to be ruler of the nations of the whole world:

> Ask me, and I will make the nations your inheritance,
> > the ends of the earth your possession. (Ps. 2:8)

> you have made me (David) the head of nations.
> > (Ps. 18:43)

> May all kings bow down to him (the King)
> > and all nations serve him...
> Then *all nations will be blessed through him*,
> > and they will call him blessed. (Ps. 72:11, 17)

These affirmations and prayers for the King in David's line have their roots in the covenant with Abraham and his seed. Notice especially the words printed in italics, which echo very closely the promise of Genesis 12:3.

Often the Psalms speak of the nations of the world or the ends of the earth as coming to join in the praise of the God of Israel. Whenever they do this, the promise to Abraham lies in the background. Here are some examples:

> …so that your ways may be known on earth,
>   your salvation among all nations.
> May the peoples praise you, God;
>   may all the peoples praise you… (Ps. 67:2-3)

> All the ends of the earth will remember and turn to
>   the LORD,
> and all the families (or 'peoples' – echoing Gen. 12:3)
>   of the nations will bow down before him
>   (Ps. 22:27)

> Rise up, O God, judge the earth,
>   for all the nations are your inheritance.
>   (Ps. 82:8)

> All the nations you have made
>   will come and worship before you, Lord…
>   (Ps. 86:9)

> The nations will fear the name of the LORD,
>   all the kings of the earth will revere your glory.
>   (Ps. 102:15)

How is the promise of covenant blessing compatible with the justice of the covenant curse?

The problem is that the second strand – curse for covenant-breaking – would seem to be incompatible with the sure promise of worldwide blessing. This problem lies at the heart of the final two Psalms in Book 4, Psalms 105 and 106.

Psalm 105 is the fullest and clearest exposition of the Abrahamic covenant in the Psalms. Near the start and end there are explicit references to the covenant and promise to Abraham:

> ...the descendants of Abraham... (v. 6)

> the covenant he made with Abraham (v. 9)

> For he remembered his holy promise
>   given to his servant Abraham (v. 42)

So, although this Psalm takes us much further in the Bible story than Abraham in Genesis, this beginning and end signal to us that the primary focus of the whole Psalm is the covenant with Abraham.

Psalms 105 and 106 are remarkably similar and yet radically different. Each tells a largely overlapping sequence from the Bible story. Psalm 105 tells extracts of the story from Abraham, through Joseph and the family coming to Egypt, their enslavement, the Exodus, and the wilderness wanderings, culminating in the gift of the Promised Land. Psalm 106 covers the period from Egypt, through the Exodus and wilderness wanderings, and finally into the Promised Land. But whereas Psalm 105 is entirely positive, Psalm 106 is deeply and soberingly negative. In it the people of God admit, 'We have sinned, even as our ancestors did' (v. 6) and tell the story as a catalogue of unbelief followed by more unbelief. It ends with the prayer:

> Save us, LORD our God,
>   and gather us from the nations... (v. 47)

We need to be gathered because we have been scattered, in the Babylonian exile.

Psalm 105 exhorts those who seek the LORD (v. 3) – that is, genuine believers – to 'remember the wonders he has done' (v. 5). These 'wonders' take us through the wanderings of the patriarchs (vv. 12-15), the rescue through Joseph from famine (vv. 16-22), redemption from slavery in Egypt (vv. 23-38), provision in the wilderness (vv. 39-41) right into the Promised Land (42-45), which is a core part of the covenant promise to Abraham. Indeed, verses 7-11 make it clear that all this history is God remembering His covenant with Abraham.

We are told that,

- God made a covenant with Abraham.

- This covenant extends, via Isaac and Jacob, to all the people of Israel. In the context of how this Psalm begins, this means those who actively seek the LORD's face with deliberate intentional faith.

- This covenant is 'forever', 'for a thousand generations' and has been 'confirmed' as a 'decree,' where the word translated 'decree' (often translated 'statute') emphasises its permanence and binding force.

- The content of the covenant is 'the land of Canaan'. The covenant promise includes other elements, as we have seen; but the emphasis here in this Psalm is on the land.

After the long and wonderful retelling of the story of covenant-keeping, there is a sting in the tail of the Psalm, in the final verse. There is a purpose in this covenant: 'that they might keep his precepts and observe his laws' (v. 45).

For what purpose did God multiply Abraham's family, protect and preserve them, redeem them, and give them the land? Or, to ask the same question more deeply, towards what goal did God make His covenant with Abraham? The answer is pregnant with both threat and hope: He did it in order to create a new humanity who would 'keep his precepts and observe his laws'. In a disordered and ugly spoiled world full of violence, hatred, sexual chaos, greed and deceit, here is to be a people shaped by the Ten Commandments into the beauty of God's order – in the objects of their worship (the first three commandments), the patterns of their week (the Sabbath), their respect for authority (the fifth commandment), their love for human beings (the sixth commandment), their honouring of the marriage of a man and a woman (the seventh commandment), their respect for property and people (the eighth commandment), their honouring of truth (the ninth commandment) and their hearts shaped by godly contentment (the tenth commandment), these people are to show the world how human beings are meant to live.

This is why we are in exile! Because we have precisely not fulfilled our side of the covenant. This is the sting in the tail of this tale! And yet this is not – cannot be – the end of the story.

We have here a covenant with a purpose. It is at the same time a definite covenant, fixed and sure – God will do what He has said He will do – and a conditional covenant that can and will only reach its fulfilment when a covenant people are created who will keep His precepts and observe His laws.

How can this happen? How can the covenant with Abraham be at the same time definite and conditional? We shall now see how the theme of the Abrahamic covenant must find its fulfilment in Jesus Christ.

How does the New Testament understand the covenant with Abraham?

The New Creation

It is important to put together this element of worldwide rule and blessing with the promise of the land. Although the Promised Land had boundaries, the assurance of final worldwide rule and blessing demonstrates that this time-and-space-limited land was but a shadow of a greater reality.

> He has shown his people the power of his works,
> giving them the lands (lit. the inheritance) of other
>   nations. (Ps. 111:6)

In the end, the worldwide rule of God through His Davidic King will mean that the territory of this King has no boundaries. Paul writes that God promised 'Abraham and his offspring' to be 'heir of *the world*' (Rom. 4:13).

And so the New Testament understands the fulfilment of the Abrahamic covenant to be the new heavens and new earth, the whole created order restored and renewed. When we read 'land' or 'inheritance' language in the Psalms, we need to remember that ultimately this is where it is pointing, to that 'inheritance…kept in heaven for you' (1 Pet. 1:4) ready to come down from heaven to earth, and to fill the whole universe as the New Creation.

Who is (or are) Abraham's 'seed'?

While it is wonderful to affirm that God keeps His promises, the really important existential question for us is, 'Who will inherit these promises?' For unless I can be confident that the promise to Abraham will benefit me, the study of it is

– at best – of antiquarian interest. There is a great danger of false assurance. People were saying to John the Baptist, 'We are alright. We do not need to repent because "We have Abraham as our father" and therefore we are safe.' To which complacent false assurance, John the Baptist replied, 'Produce fruit in keeping with repentance (i.e. the repentance you profess but do not actually have). And do not begin to say to yourselves, "We have Abraham as our father." For I tell you that out of these stones God can raise up children for Abraham' (Luke 3:8). They said the same to Jesus: 'Abraham is our father' (John 8:39); to which hypocrisy Jesus spoke some pretty challenging truths about their true spiritual paternity (John 8:39-44)!

So true repentance that bears fruit in a changed life is a mark of being a spiritual child of Abraham. Ongoing daily repentance is the flip side of faith. Galatians 3:10-14 and Romans 4 are two of the most important New Testament passages expounding the Abrahamic covenant in the light of Christ. Romans 4 teaches that it is people with faith in Christ who are Abraham's true children. Galatians 3:10-14 teaches that because Jesus bore the curse of the covenant for all who would trust in Him, 'the blessing given (that is, promised) to Abraham might come to the Gentiles through Christ Jesus, so that by faith we might receive the promise of the Spirit.' The promise to Abraham is given to all who trust in Jesus' curse-bearing death for them, and who thereby receive the Spirit. They are destined to govern the world with Jesus (1 Cor. 6:2); as forgiven sinners by the Cross, they begin – by the Spirit – to be made 'fit for purpose' as godly governors.

How is the Abrahamic covenant to be fulfilled? Not through people who stubbornly claim to be children of Abraham despite all the evidence to the contrary (Luke 3:8-9;

John 8:39). But by people whose sin has been paid for by the curse-bearing Saviour and who, through and in this Saviour, receive the Holy Spirit to begin to change their hearts (Gal. 3:10-14). It is through this Christ and this Spirit that the blessing promised to Abraham finally spreads through all the world as even Gentiles are brought into the covenant people.

Mostly in the Psalms, the Abrahamic covenant is in the deep background rather than explicit in the foreground. But it is very significant deep background, for the simple reason that God made a promise, and God will keep every promise He made.

11. Exodus in the Psalms

If the covenant with Abraham guarantees that God will do what He has promised to do, the events of the Exodus put that promise into practice; they provide us with the definitive redemption that guarantees the final rest of the people of God.

The Exodus events

By 'the events of the Exodus' I mean the whole sequence that begins with God's people in slavery in Egypt and ends with them possessing the Promised Land, with one huge exception: Sinai. The mountain of Sinai casts a tremendous shadow over all the Pentateuch; the ways in which it impacts the Psalms will be the subject of the next chapter. In this chapter we consider how the following events are remembered, reflected upon, celebrated, or used in prayer or praise in the Psalms:

- God's people languishing in slavery in Egypt

- …and calling out to the LORD from their slavery (Exod. 2:23-25)

- The LORD judging the Pharaoh and his forces with the plagues

- …and finally the death of the firstborn

- The crossing of the Red Sea and the defeat of Pharaoh

- The wilderness wanderings and the LORD's protection and provision

In short, this bringing *out* (of Egypt), bringing *through* (the wilderness) and bringing *in* (to the land) may be referred to by the umbrella heading of the Exodus events.

The Exodus events remembered in the Psalms
The song by the Red Sea (Exod. 15) is the first Psalm. It gives the definitive pattern for celebrating the Exodus and is frequently echoed later in the Old Testament (think, for example, of how 'the horse and his rider' appears elsewhere).

The Exodus is often in the background when fairly general language is used of God in the Psalms. Here are some examples:

- The 'mighty acts' of the LORD, His 'wonders,' His 'wonderful works', or His 'great deeds' (e.g. Ps. 145:3-12). This language may refer to Creation, but often – perhaps usually – refers primarily to the Exodus events.

- The LORD's 'mighty hand' and/or His 'outstretched arm' (e.g. Ps. 136:12, echoing, for example, Deut. 5:15)

- References to 'redemption' or the LORD 'redeeming' (e.g. Ps. 26:11 'deliver me' in NIV)

- The LORD bringing people 'out' (e.g. Ps. 68:6 'he leads *out* the prisoners with singing')

- God's people crying out to Him in trouble (e.g. Ps. 145:19 'hears their cry,' echoing Exod. 2:23-25)

- Times when the Psalmists' troubles are described in terms of waters, the sea, the deep, torrents, or floods (e.g. Ps. 18:4)

- When the Psalmists celebrate that God is their 'Rock' (e.g. Ps. 18:2) echoing the repetition of this word in Deuteronomy 32, the Song that Moses taught the people on the edge of the Promised Land.

The more sustained references to the Exodus appear in Books 3, 4, and 5 of the Psalter. Here are the main occurrences of the theme in Book 3:

- Psalm 74 (v. 2 'the nation you *purchased* – redeemed – long ago'; v. 13 'you...split open the sea').

- Psalm 77, where 'the former days, the years of long ago' (v. 5) or 'the years when the Most High stretched out his *right hand*' (v. 10) refer primarily to the Exodus, as we see in verses 10-20. Notice, for example, 'with your *mighty arm* you *redeemed* your people' (v. 15) and 'The waters saw you...and writhed' (v. 16). And there are echoes of the Song by the Sea in Exodus 15.

- The historical overview in Psalm 78 majors on the events of the Exodus and the wilderness wanderings

that followed. See, for example, 'He did miracles...
in the land of Egypt' (v. 12), 'he divided the sea and
led them through' (v. 13), 'He struck down all the
firstborn of Egypt' (v. 51), 'he brought his people
out' (v. 52).

- Psalm 80:8-11 describes the Exodus and the
  settlement of the Promised Land in terms of the
  LORD transplanting 'a vine from Egypt' and then
  planting it in the Promised Land.

- Psalm 81 remembers 'When God went out against
  Egypt' (v. 5) and 'removed the burden from their
  shoulders' (v. 6), because 'In your distress you called
  and I rescued you' (v. 7).

In Book 4 there is a brief mention of the 'pillar of cloud' in
Psalm 99:7. But there are two Psalms in which the Exodus
features significantly:

- Psalm 105 where, as we have seen in chapter 10,
  verses 23-44 set the whole Exodus sequence in
  the context of the LORD keeping His promise to
  Abraham.

- Psalm 106:7-33, where the focus is on the people's
  sinful unbelief in the face of these wonderful
  events.

In Book 5, three Psalms explicitly remember the Exodus:

- Psalm 114 begins, 'When Israel came out of Egypt'
  and the whole Psalm reflects on the Exodus.

- Psalm 135:8-12 begins with the striking down of
  'the firstborn of Egypt' (v. 8) and continues this

theme of the LORD striking down His enemies all the way to the Promised Land.

- Psalm 136:10-24 similarly celebrates the LORD demonstrating His covenant love ('His love endures for ever') as He strikes down the firstborn of Egypt (v. 10), brings Israel out (v. 11), 'with a mighty hand and outstretched arm' (v. 12), divides the Red Sea (vv. 13-15) and leads His people through the wilderness (vv. 16-20) until finally He brings His people into the land (vv. 21-24).

The Significance of the Exodus in the Psalms

Apart from training ourselves to pick up the allusions or references to the Exodus events, the really important question is this: Why do the Psalmists keep alluding to the Exodus? What do they learn – and want us to learn – from these events? I think we may summarise the main lessons under three headings. First, the Exodus shows the Creator restoring Creation Order through the redemption of His people and the conquest of evil. It therefore, second, reveals the Covenant God in all His covenant love and power. Finally, because it reveals the character of God, it becomes the paradigm for redemption, a revelation of God that grounds hope for future acts of redemption. We shall consider these in turn.

The Exodus shows the Creator restoring Creation Order through the Redemption of His people and the Conquest of evil

The critical theme is water. Creation begins with darkness on the face of 'the deep' and the Spirit of God over 'the waters' (Gen. 1:2). God separates the waters, so that there are waters under the sky and waters above the sky, and the waters under the sky are gathered together so that dry ground can exist (Genesis 1:6-10). Water must be pushed to the edges so that dry land can exist and animal and human life exist and flourish. Flood waters threaten human life and the goodness of the Creator is shown in the way He makes and guards a sphere of solid, dry, reliable ground in which life can flourish (and indeed in the way He makes flood waters into rain water which actually nourishes life). We have seen this in chapter 9.

At the Exodus the people of God are threatened (see Exod. 14) by forces of death behind them (Pharaoh's army) and in front of them (the waters of the Red Sea). The song of Exodus 15 majors on language of water: 'the sea...the Red Sea...the deep waters...the depths...the waters... the surging waters...the deep waters...in the heart of the sea' (Exod. 15:4, 5, 8, 10). These waters are physical, but not merely physical; they are the material manifestation of spiritual forces of darkness. The battle is not simply between Israel's God and Pharaoh's army. The victory that the LORD wins is over 'all the *gods* of Egypt' (Exod. 12:12). This is a supernatural battle. The LORD drives back the waters of death so that the people can pass through on dry ground (Exod. 14:21-22). He does something very similar on the edge of the Promised Land when He enables them to cross the Jordan 'on dry ground' (Josh. 3:17). Both actions of God are reminiscent of Creation. Sometimes in the Psalms the themes of Exodus and Creation echo around one another. One example is Psalm 74. In verse 13 the Psalmist says, 'It was you who split open the sea by your power' and we immediately think he is remembering the crossing of the Red Sea. But as we read through verses 13-17 we find it is primarily about creation (see especially verses 16-17 with their references to day and night, sun and moon, the boundaries of the earth, summer and winter).

This connection between Exodus and Creation is very significant. It means that Redemption is integrally tied to the restoration of Creation Order. When God acts to redeem His people, He is doing something much bigger than just rescuing an apparently randomly-selected group; He is beginning a process, the culmination of which will be the restoration of perfect order in a world that has been invaded by the forces of chaos and darkness. The goal of the Exodus is far bigger than just a patch of land in what we now call the Middle East; it is the new heavens and the new earth, in which righteousness will dwell (2 Pet. 3).

The Exodus therefore reveals the Covenant love and power of God

Precisely because Redemption recapitulates Creation, the Redeemer is never to be separated from the Creator. The religions of the ancient near east might have distinguished between the most high God El, who would be credited with creation, and other gods or goddesses, perhaps Ba'al, who might act in history or nature. But the Bible insists there is one God, who is both Creator and Redeemer. It follows that the great redemptive act of the Exodus reveals the character of the Creator God. In particular it unveils His love and His power. In their reflections on the Exodus, the Psalms draw out precisely these qualities of God: He is the God of covenant love and He puts that covenant love into practice with invincible power.

Psalm 135 illustrates this. After calling us to praise and declaring that 'the LORD is good,' (v. 3) the Psalmist declares,

I know that the LORD is great,
   that our Lord is greater than all gods.
The LORD does whatever pleases him,
   in the heavens and on the earth,
   in the seas and all their depths. (vv. 5,6).

(Notice that explicit inclusion of the seas and their depths.)

The Psalm goes on to remember the events of the Exodus in verses 8-12. This covenant God who is both 'good' and 'great' has demonstrated His goodness and His greatness in the Exodus.

The refrain in Psalm 136, 'His (covenant steadfast) love endures for ever' presents the Exodus as a demonstration of that covenant love.

The Exodus therefore becomes the paradigm
for Redemption and the revelation of God that
grounds hope for future Redemption

Because the Exodus events reveal God in His unchanging covenant goodness and greatness, it follows that the Exodus is more than a wonderful 'one off' sequence; rather it gives the standard 'shape' in which God acts in redemption and therefore gives solid grounds for the people of God in troubles to hope for future Exodus-like redemptions.

This paradigmatic role of the Exodus is indicated right at the start, by the surprising content of the second half of the song in Exodus 15. Verses 2-10 celebrate the great deliverance of the Crossing of the Red Sea. Verse 11 reflects that this demonstrates the unique holy majesty of the LORD, the Covenant God. We can understand how they would rejoice in the past deliverance they have just experienced. But in the remainder of the Psalm they rejoice in a rescue not yet experienced. The enemies in verses 12-17 – Philistia,

Edom, Moab, and Canaan – have not yet been encountered, let alone defeated. It is a strange truth of this song that past good news becomes the key to future confidence. This is not usually the case in human affairs. A child may have excellent exam results from last year; it is no guarantee of success this year. An athlete may have won gold at the Olympics four years ago; but they have to fight all the way to win gold again. You may have succeeded at your last job; but when you start a new one, you have to prove yourself all over again. And yet, in the gospel foreshadowed in the Exodus, a past deliverance is the key to future assurance.

On what basis can they celebrate being brought right in to the Promised Land (v. 17)? On the basis of the covenant faithfulness and unbeatable covenant power of the Redeemer demonstrated in the Exodus. The conclusion is therefore that the LORD does not just reign this time around, for this battle, rather as England keep celebrating winning the World Cup in 1966, rather sadly having to pass over all the subsequent failures. No, the LORD reigns for ever and ever. This decisive victory in some way guarantees the eternal victory and rule of the covenant God.

We see this paradigmatic role of the Exodus especially in Psalms that are stirred by the Babylonian Exile (see chapter 14), and most especially in Book 3 (see Pss. 74, 77, 78, 80, and 81). For example, in Psalm 77 the troubled Psalmist thinks, 'To this I will appeal' (v. 10) and then appeals precisely to the Exodus Redemption. He understands that the God who showed Himself to be Redeemer at the Exodus is the same God today.

Perhaps the clearest example of the Exodus being the grounds for future hope is in Psalm 81 (not least because it comes from the voice of God). The voice that says,

'I removed the burden from their shoulders,' that repeats that covenant formula 'I am the LORD your God who brought you up out of Egypt' (cf. Exod. 20:1), that reminds them of Exodus mercies (vv. 6, 7, 10), is the voice that then appeals to them to present-tense repentance and faith and offers them the promise, 'Open wide your mouth and I will fill it' and 'you would be filled with the finest of wheat; with honey from the rock I would satisfy you' (vv. 10, 16). 'If only my people would listen to me,' says the LORD, how much I would do another Exodus-type redeeming act for them. But they must listen!

How does the New Testament teach us to understand the Exodus?
It may be helpful to give just three salient points to help us draw persuasive lines from the Exodus to Christ.

The Passover Lamb of the Exodus is fulfilled in the Cross of Christ
In Luke's account of the Transfiguration of Jesus there is a suggestive hint. Moses and Elijah appear, 'talking with Jesus. They spoke about his departure' – that is, literally, His Exodus – 'which he was about to bring to fulfilment at Jerusalem' (Luke 9:30-31). This is at the very least a hint that on the Cross Jesus would bring to fulfilment what is prefigured in the Exodus events.

Paul explicitly writes that 'Christ, our Passover lamb, has been sacrificed' (1 Cor. 5:7). The judgment of God upon sinners, that fell upon the Egypt of the Pharaohs in the deaths of the firstborn, passed over the people of God only if they smeared their doorposts with the blood of the Passover lamb. The symbolism of substitution is very clear: the death of the lamb takes the place of the death of the firstborn. Christ is that Passover lamb; it is by His death that He bears the just judgment of God against His sinful people and enables the whole of the Exodus drama to be fulfilled in them.

The conquest of evil in the Exodus is fulfilled in the Cross of Christ

One of the great emphases in the telling and retellings of the Exodus story is that it shows the very great power of God to destroy the powers of death and evil that threaten His people. The Exodus is a great victory. This conquest, foreshadowed in the Exodus, is fulfilled at the Cross of Jesus, in which 'by his death' He broke 'the power of him who holds the power of death – that is, the devil' (Heb. 2:14); by His death He 'disarmed the (hostile) powers and authorities… made a public spectacle of them, triumphing over them by the cross' (Col. 2:15). Just as God made a public spectacle of Pharaoh's army and broke their death-giving power, so – in a greater fulfilment – He made a public spectacle of the devil and all his armies at the cross of Christ.

The New Testament takes the definitive victory of the Exodus and teaches that it foreshadows the utterly definitive victory of the Cross. Because the Cross of Christ establishes the victory of God over the powers of evil, that past rescue – to which we look whenever we celebrate the Lord's Supper – gives us the grounds for future confidence. They praised God for the Exodus because it guaranteed the Promised Land; Christians praise God for the Cross of Christ because it guarantees the New Creation. We may be sure that the God who has given us Jesus will, with Jesus, give us all things necessary for final salvation (Rom. 8:32). Because, on the cross, Jesus took the sting of death, which is sin, by bearing the curse, the day will surely come when death will be swallowed up in victory (1 Cor. 15:54-57).

Jesus Christ the Son of God is the New Moses
who sets His people free from slavery to sin
It follows that Jesus Christ the Son of God is the one who does what Moses only foreshadowed. Moses led the people of God out of slavery to Pharaoh; Jesus the Son of God leads the people of God out of slavery to sin. 'Very truly I tell you, everyone who sins is a slave to sin...' but 'if the Son sets you free, you will be free indeed' (John 8:34-36).

In these three ways – true sacrifice, true victory, and true freedom – Jesus Christ fulfils all that the Exodus foreshadows.

12. Sinai in the Psalms

The Pentateuch spans from the Creation of the world to the death of Moses; of this vast expanse of time, the people of Israel spent less than one year at Sinai (see Exod. 19 with Num. 1:1 and 10:11). Yet what happened at that mountain fills one third of these five books. It is as if 'time wraps around Mount Sinai.'[11] As Israel gathers by the mountain of God they hear ten words (the Ten Commandments), just as there were ten words ('and God said') at the Creation of the world (Gen. 1:3, 6, 9, 11, 14, 20, 24, 26, 28, 29). The giving of the law is an event comparable with the creation of the world (cf. Deut. 4:32-33).[12] And yet, perhaps to our surprise, there are very few explicit mentions of Sinai in the Psalms. But Sinai lies behind much of the Psalms, as we shall see.

---

11. Burnside 2011:45.
12. Burnside 2011:52.

In the previous chapter we considered what I called in shorthand 'the events of the Exodus,' meaning everything that happened to Israel from slavery in Egypt to the occupation of the Promised Land. I excluded Sinai because the impact of Old Covenant Law on the Psalms deserves a separate chapter.

We consider the subject under four headings, with a simple logical structure. We begin with the character of God as holy; we move from there to the necessary entailment, that there is blessing in a holy life and curse on a wicked life. From there we deduce two contrasting responses. The first is penitence and the yearning for forgiveness; the second is the life of faith, shaped and directed by the Law of God.

The Psalms revere God in His moral holiness as revealed at Sinai

Israel never forgot the day recorded in Exodus 19 when the mountain flamed with fire, when God in His holiness descended on the mountain. As Psalm 68 puts it,

> the earth shook, the heavens poured down rain,
> before God, the One of Sinai... (Ps. 68:8)

The God of Sinai is 'enthroned as the Holy One' (Ps. 22:3). Three times Psalm 99 affirms, 'He is holy' (vv. 3, 5, 9). 'Holy and awesome is his name' (Ps. 111:9). He is 'seated on his holy throne' (Ps. 47:8), as 'the Holy One of Israel' (e.g. Ps. 71:22). His 'arm' (i.e. actions) is holy (Ps. 98:1) as are His 'ways' (Ps. 77:13); His name (character) is holy (e.g. Ps. 30:4 and many others), the mountain where He dwells (Zion) is holy (e.g. Ps. 2:6 and many others), because His house or temple is holy (e.g. Ps. 5:7), His 'place' is holy (e.g. Ps. 24:3), and His whole land is therefore 'the holy land'

(Ps. 78:54). His character and name is holy, and therefore His Spirit is most deeply holy (Ps. 51:11).

The Ten Commandments at Sinai make it very clear that the LORD's holiness is more than just an awesome power that evokes a reaction of numinous awe. Holiness is moral. The answer to the question, 'LORD, who may dwell in your sacred tent? Who may live on your holy mountain?' is not 'the mystic' but 'the one whose way of life is blameless, who does what is righteous, who speaks the truth from their heart…' (Ps. 15:1-2). David is deeply conscious of the *Holy* Spirit of the LORD in Psalm 51 because he has sinned (Ps. 51:11).

The Psalms affirm the covenant blessings and curses revealed at Sinai

Because God, who is Creator and Sustainer of life, is holy, only the one who walks in holiness of life can enjoy fellowship with Him and know the blessing of life. The covenant blessings (for covenant faithfulness to God) and curses (for covenant unfaithfulness) follow necessarily from the holy name of the covenant God.

This truth is placed at the very front door of the Psalter. Psalms 1 and 2 are a clear 'front door' marker to the Psalter. Psalm 2 speaks of the covenant with the Davidic King (see chapter 13). Psalm 1 proclaims in a clear voice right at the beginning of the Psalms that there is blessing for the one who turns from sin and delights in the law of the LORD, and there must necessarily be curse for those who do not.

This truth is affirmed repeatedly. Psalm 15 teaches clearly that only the one whose way of life is blameless will dwell in the presence of God. Psalm 24 similarly asks,

> Who may ascend the mountain of the LORD?
> Who may stand in his *holy* place?

and answers,

> The one who has clean hands and a pure heart…
> (vv. 3,4)

The Psalms cling to this truth even when the evidence around seems to contradict it. Most famously, in Psalm 73 the Psalmist struggles with the prosperity of the wicked (v. 3), which seems to contradict Psalm 1 – and indeed the promised blessings and curses of the covenant. And yet he still affirms at the start that,

> Surely God is good…to those who are pure in heart.
> (v. 1)

where the word 'surely' has the force of a creedal affirmation[13] – 'God really is good to those who are pure in heart, despite the evidence to the contrary.'

Near the end – again with that word 'surely' – we see the flip side, that

> Surely you place them on slippery ground;
> you cast them down to ruin. (v. 18)

and,

> Those who are far from you will perish;
> you destroy all who are unfaithful to you. (v. 27)

Near the end of the Psalter the same truth is affirmed, after all the troubles of Israel's history, that

> The LORD watches over all who love him,
> but all the wicked he will destroy. (Ps. 145:20)

And again in Psalm 146,

---

13. J. L. Crenshaw, quoted in Grogan 2008:259.

the LORD loves the righteous…
but he frustrates the ways of the wicked. (Ps. 146:8-9)

Perhaps most significantly of all, Psalm 16 expresses the confidence that flows from righteousness of life. David claims a deep, wholehearted, consistent, and sustained loyalty to the LORD. As a result, he is sure he will be safe even in the face of death. We have seen that he speaks by the Spirit of a later believer who will truly be all that David wanted to be. There is one who fulfils the ideal of Psalm 1, but only one. Only Jesus Christ is the truly and perfectly righteous one, and therefore by nature the heir to the covenant blessings.

The Psalms know deeply the need of forgiveness and hold on to the covenant promises of forgiveness fulfilled in Christ

'Through the law we become conscious of our sin' (Rom. 3:20). This is deeply true of the Psalms. When the Psalmists lament their sin and the burden of the wrath of God, they are affirming the truth of Sinai, of the Old Covenant, of the Holiness of God. This so-called 'religious' use of the Law is modelled for us most intensely in the Psalms.

Psalm 19 celebrates how the Created Order speaks of the glory of God (vv. 1-6) and goes on to celebrate the perfections and beauty of the Law of God (vv. 7-11). But as David meditates on the purity of the Law, and the purity of the LORD whom the Law reveals, he is convicted of sin. The Law warns him (v. 11). He responds by crying out,

But who can discern their own errors?
Forgive my hidden faults.

Keep your servant also from wilful sins;
may they not rule over me… (vv. 12-13)

Psalm 32 celebrates the blessings of forgiveness. But perhaps the most revealing example is in Psalm 103, verses 7-12. The Psalm begins with heartfelt praise for all the LORD's benefits, and in particular for the forgiveness of sins and therefore hope in the face of death ('the pit') (vv. 1-5). But how do we know – how can David know – that the LORD forgives sins? After all, does not the Sinai covenant proclaim His holiness and the necessary curse upon covenant-breakers? The passage that follows takes us back to a terrible sequence of events immediately following the revelation of the covenant at Sinai. Exodus 32 records how, while Moses was with God on Mount Sinai, the people made for themselves a golden calf to worship in the context of immorality and idolatry. As Moses intercedes for the people, he prays, 'If you are pleased with me, teach me your ways…' (Exod. 33:13). The Psalm remembers the answer to that prayer. Astonishingly, the pure and holy God is

> compassionate and gracious,
> slow to anger, abounding in (covenant) love. (v. 8)

This echoes closely the answer to Moses prayer in Exodus 34:6.[14]

> The LORD, the LORD,
> the compassionate and gracious God,
> slow to anger, abounding in love and faithfulness…

This is the most quoted verse of scripture within scripture. It echoes around the chambers of the word of God from book to book. Elsewhere in the Psalms, here are two examples:

> But you, Lord, are a compassionate and gracious God,
> slow to anger, abounding in love and faithfulness.
>   (Ps. 86:15)

---

14. Kirkpatrick.

> The LORD is gracious and compassionate,
> slow to anger and rich in love. (Ps. 145:8)

In Psalm 103, verse 8 picks up those first four descriptions – compassionate, gracious, slow to anger, abounding in (covenant steadfast) love. Verses 9-12 go on to celebrate the consequences of this character, and these ways, of the LORD. The key word, repeated in verse 11, is covenant love (*chesed*). One of the paradoxes of the Old Covenant was that it continued in spite of repeated grievous covenant-breaking. Although it was a conditional covenant, whose blessings came only through covenant faithfulness, nevertheless it contained an unconditional promise: these blessings will come. This paradox could not be resolved until 'the (covenant) obedience of the one man' should 'make many righteous' (Rom. 5:19).

The basis of forgiveness lies, not in us, but in the faithful steadfast covenant love of God. Our sin, like that of Israel with the golden calf, is inexcusable. And yet God forgives. We now know what David could not know, except in the most shadowy way: how the righteous God could be at the same time 'just' (the just judge) and 'the one who justifies those who have faith in Jesus.' We know how God could leave 'the sins committed beforehand unpunished' for all who trusted His covenant promise. This wonderful forgiveness, claimed by David and all who truly believed the Old Covenant promises, was possible only because the Lord Jesus Christ would die to be the propitiation for sins (Rom. 3:21-26). He is the man of Psalm 1 who inherits the blessing of the covenant; we are the wicked of Psalm 1 who deserve the curses of the covenant. By His substitutionary death He becomes the curse for us (Gal. 3:13), so that we may inherit His blessing. The Psalmists knew this only hazily, but they did know it (1 Peter 1:10-12). When we pray these Psalms in Christ we do so according to the true and original meaning of the Psalms, made clear now Christ has come.

The Psalms include the voice of Torah instruction to guide the believer in the life of faith

Psalm 105 concludes that the goal of the Exodus events and the Abrahamic covenant was 'that they might keep his precepts and observe his laws' (Ps. 105:45). The goal of salvation is that there should be a people who bear the image of God by living God's way and sharing God's heart. While the Law brings conviction of sin and brings home to our hearts our need of a Saviour, this is not its final purpose. Its goal is to shape a people according to the heart and character of God.[15]

Because Old Covenant believers were justified by God's grace through faith and received His righteousness, it was possible for them to have some real experience of delighting in God's law (see chapter 5). Although by nature there is one, and only one, man who fulfils the ideal of Psalm 1, nevertheless there were others in the Old Covenant era, sinful men and women, but genuine believers; they genuinely feared the LORD and loved His law.

When David says, 'your law is within my heart' (Ps. 40:8 and cf. Ps. 37:31), this is fulfilled in Jesus Christ, as Hebrews 10:5-7 teaches. But there was some sense in which the Spirit of Jesus could work in the hearts of the

---

15. Gordon Wenham has argued persuasively for the ways the Psalms make use of the Ten Commandments. See 'The Ethics of the Psalms' in Johnston and Firth 2005:179-187.

Psalmists, so that they could truly claim that the Law of God was written upon their hearts. They could truly delight in the Law of God, as Psalm 1 exhorted them to do. The full flowering of this law written on the heart would not – could not –come until Christ had died and the New Covenant been inaugurated (see Heb. 10), but there were anticipations in the Spirit-inspired prophetic writings which were the Psalms. Psalm 119 is the most beautiful and sustained example of this genuine law-loving piety.[16]

It follows that what we sometimes call 'the Third Use of the Law' (to guide Spirit-led believers in living to please God) has its place in the Psalms of Instruction. These are the Psalms – or places within the Psalms – where we hear the voice of God's instruction through God's leader or King, teaching the people of God how to live. Their style is didactic; the voice we hear is the voice of God instructing His people. Examples include Psalms 1, 25:8-10, 32:8-11, 37, 49, 78, 92:12-15, 94:8-15, 111:2-10, and 112. Jesus twice quotes from the Psalms while calling it 'Law' (John 10:34 and 15:25). We have seen (chapter 3) that in Psalm 78 the voice of the teacher is fulfilled in the teaching ministry of Christ, who is the Father's mouthpiece (Matt. 13:35).

Conclusion

When we hear the character of God extolled as holy, the blessing of God promised to the righteous, a curse pronounced upon the wicked, forgiveness offered to the penitent, and the way of godliness taught by instruction, Mount Sinai is there in the background. Sinai may not be mentioned explicitly very often in the Psalms, but its influence is everywhere.

---

16. see Ash 2008.

13. Zion in the Psalms

We move now from one mountain, Sinai, to another mountain, Zion, from a mountain that inspires fear to a mountain that attracts worldwide love. Hebrews 12:18-29 would be a good commentary on this transition!

Overview

Whenever the Psalms speak – as they often do – of Zion, Jerusalem, or the LORD's 'house' or 'temple,' they key in to a whole raft of Bible truth. At the heart of this is the covenant with David. Supremely Zion is the city of David (2 Sam. 5:7 'the fortress of Zion – which is the City of David'). If Psalm 1 affirms Sinai holiness, Psalm 2 speaks of kingly promise. God says, 'I have installed my king on Zion, my holy mountain' (Ps. 2:6). King and Temple are the twin pillars of Zion. Psalm 68 begins with words that echo Numbers 10:35, 'May God arise, may his enemies be scattered'. With these words the Ark of the Covenant used to lead the people into battle. Psalm 68 would appear to celebrate the bringing of the Ark in to Jerusalem (2 Sam. 6), the event that is immediately followed by the LORD making His covenant with David (2 Sam. 7).

Zion, the City of David, is the place where God dwells on earth. God lives in the highest heaven, but His feet touch earth in Zion where His King reigns and His Temple stands (cf. Pss. 9:11, 11:4, 132:13-14). In Psalm 99 Zion is described, in parallel terms, as 'his holy mountain' (v. 9) and 'his footstool' (v. 5).

Zion was the focus of the covenant promises and the final goal of the Exodus:

You will bring them in and plant them
　　on the mountain of your inheritance –
the place, LORD, you made for your dwelling,
　　the sanctuary, LORD, your hands established.
　　　　(Exod. 15:17)

Because the LORD dwells in Zion it is 'the city of God'
(e.g. Psalm 46:4).

Significance: where is Zion today?[17]

Zion is so common in the Psalms that it is of the utmost
importance we should develop a proper biblical understanding
of where and how Zion is fulfilled in the New Covenant. We
need a biblical theology of Zion so that we can transpose
Zion language from its Old Covenant context in the Psalms
into the New Covenant setting in which Christians live today.
Jerusalem in Bible language was not only a physical place but
also meant something; what it meant did not correspond
with what it was actually like on the ground. When we read
the language of Jerusalem in our Bibles today, what should
we be thinking about? What does the writer of the letter to
the Hebrews mean by saying to Christian people that when
they assemble for church they 'have come to Mount Zion, to
the heavenly Jerusalem' (Heb. 12:22)?

　　Here are four pointers. The first is a necessary negative.
The second, third and fourth are positive.

Zion is not in the Middle East.

In Old Testament times, Jerusalem was quite simply and
literally a place, a city. You could find it on a map. You can
find where it *was*, in a Bible atlas. But Jerusalem in a Bible
atlas, or Jerusalem the capital of the state of Israel, is not

---

17. This section is adapted from Ash 2010:80-83.

the same as Jerusalem in new covenant Bible significance. When today under the new covenant we speak of Jerusalem, we are not speaking of travelling to the Middle East. If we were, then Christianity would be an elite religion in which those who could afford the tours were more privileged than those poor Christians who could not. But Christianity is the very opposite of an elite religion.

The reason Jerusalem now does not have the significance of Jerusalem then is very simple: what made Jerusalem significant then was the Temple, the place on earth where God dwelt. But in A.D. 70 the Temple was destroyed. Indeed the New Testament speaks sadly of the physical Jerusalem after Jesus; it even calls it the place of judgment, the place of spiritual slavery (Gal. 4:25).

All through Israel's history there was this tension between Jerusalem spoken of in faith, and the historical reality. Gradually they began to grasp that the physical Jerusalem, like everything else in the old covenant, was but a shadow pointing forward to a substantial reality to be revealed later.

Zion is fulfilled in the Lord Jesus Christ

Supremely Zion meant what the Temple meant, the presence of God on earth, the one place on earth where human beings could meet God without being burnt alive. But 2,000 years ago one who is greater than the Temple stood on earth (Matt. 12:6). He 'made his dwelling among us' (literally 'tabernacled among us', fulfilling what the Tabernacle had meant in the wilderness, John 1:14). Jesus spoke of His body as a 'Temple' that would be destroyed and then 'rebuilt' in three days (John 2:19-22). On the Cross He was the place where sinful human beings can meet with God without being destroyed; all that Jerusalem symbolised is fulfilled in Jesus. He is the place where we meet God, the place where we are secure, and the place where God's King rules on earth.

Zion is foreshadowed in the local church

What Zion means is anticipated now on earth in the local church. Jesus is to be found now on earth where His people gather. They, corporately as local churches, are God's Temple (1 Cor. 3:16), the place where God dwells among His people by His Spirit. (The individual Christian's body is also called a 'temple of the Holy Spirit' as an incentive to sexual purity in 1 Cor. 6:19, but the major emphasis is corporate rather than individual – for example, 2 Cor. 6:16; Eph. 2:21-22.) They are being built into a spiritual house, a temple (1 Pet. 2:5). And therefore, by the Spirit of God, the local church is a partial fulfilment of 'Jerusalem.' It is a local expression and foretaste, an anticipation, a foreshadowing, a partial but real expression of 'Jerusalem' here on earth.

Zion is waiting to come down from heaven to fill the earth

Hebrews 12 speaks of coming to 'the heavenly Jerusalem' (v. 22). One day the real and final Jerusalem will come down from heaven to earth (Rev. 21:2), fill the earth, and be the New Creation.

So Zion, or Jerusalem, is focussed on Jesus, anticipated and partially experienced in the local church, and will be fully and finally experienced in the New Creation.

Affection for Zion

One of the most significant influences of the Psalms, so far as Zion is concerned, is to stir the people of God to a lively affection and love directed towards it. We feel this affection in Psalm 84, where believers sing 'How lovely is your dwelling-place...' and yearn to be there, for their 'hearts are set on pilgrimage' (NRSV 'in whose heart are the highways to Zion'). What gets these believers out of bed in the morning is the thought of making the journey to Zion; this is the focus of their affection and the core of their desire. We find the same warmth in Psalm 126 ('When the LORD restored the fortunes of Zion, we were like those who dreamed...') and other Psalms such as 46 and 48.

This warm affection suffuses Psalm 87 perhaps more than any other. This is the Psalm that inspired John Newton to write the hymn, 'Glorious things of thee are spoken, Zion city of our God.' (And Newton understood that any believer in Christ can sing that he or she is, by grace, a member of Zion's city.) The Psalm raises the question of where your or my favourite place might be. Each of us has places that are special, perhaps because of the memories associated with them. Deeper still is the question of citizenship. All over the world, men and women in one place long to become citizens of a better country; many take huge risks to try to achieve that goal. This Psalm sets before us the country or city to which every human being ought most deeply to long to belong: Zion, fulfilled in the Church of Jesus Christ, and finally in the New Jerusalem.

It was a Psalm first sung when the assembly of the people of God was not visibly glorious, probably during or just after the Exile (the main context of Book 3). Calvin says,

> The miserable and distressing condition in which the Church was placed after the Babylonish captivity, might

be apt to sink the minds of the godly into despondency; and accordingly, the Holy Spirit here promises her restoration in a wonderful... manner, so that nothing would be more desirable than to be reckoned among the number of her members.[18]

They sang this song of Zion precisely at the time when it was not visibly true. We must learn to do the same.

The Psalm celebrates the security of the city (vv. 1,2); it is 'founded' (i.e. secure) and loved by God. In His love rests its security. The physical Jerusalem is very insecure, but there is another city, to which Jerusalem points, which is completely safe. The foundations of Zion rest on the covenant love of the LORD. If you and I are members of the Church of Christ, we are in a society loved from all eternity by the electing and unbreakable love of the Father. You are part of a city whose builder and maker is God (Heb. 11). You have a security your family, husband, wife or parents can never give you, a security your work can never give you, nor your Facebook friends, nor your real friends, nor any human society on earth, except the Church of Jesus Christ.

The Psalm goes on to rejoice that men and women from all over the world will be enrolled as Zion's citizens (vv. 3-7). The glory of Zion (v. 3 'Glorious things are said of you') is not its visible grandeur, for Zion was a burned-out ruin and then – after the exile – a rather pathetic imitation of past glories (cf. Hag. 2:3). Glory is not visible in Zion; but it is *spoken* of Zion in gospel promise.

'Zion's splendour will be its King and its roll of citizens.'[19] Rahab, the storybook monster, became a nickname for

18. Calvin.

19. Kidner 1973-5:315.

ancient Egypt (Ps. 89:10, Isa. 30:7, 51:9-10, Job 26:12). Babylon is the power that took them into exile. Philistia was an ancient enemy. Tyre with its wealth offered a seductive idolatry on the edge of the Promised Land. Cush (Upper Egypt) is remote. And yet men and women from these unlikely places will be enrolled as citizens of Zion.

These people had a natural birth, by which they were enemies of God. And yet God will give them spiritual birth, new birth, birth from above, and give them a new birth certificate marked 'Born in Zion.'

I used to live in the heart of London, a city to which the nations of the world come. Walk the streets and you hear hundreds of languages. But it is a spoiled city, a greedy city, a city of inequality and loneliness. It does not have the glory of Zion, the church of Christ. For in that city men and women who are enemies, idolaters, strangers to God, are given citizenship, and even given birth-rights. For birth is deeper than citizenship. When Paul was challenged as to the status of his Roman citizenship, he had only to say, 'But I was born a citizen' (Acts 22:28) and no further questions were asked. I was born in London; no one can contest my claim to be a Londoner.

But by grace and by the supernatural work of the Spirit of God I was born again in Zion. The glory of the Church of Christ is the glory of its wide diversity (including 'Cush'), its members who were formerly so hostile ('Rahab/Egypt,' 'Babylon' and 'Philistia') and the conversion of greedy idolaters (of which 'Tyre' is a fitting symbol). 'The LORD will write in the register of the peoples, "This one was born in Zion".' That is a wonderful picture: The sovereign God is – as it were – sitting in eternal wisdom and glory, at His desk with the book of life before Him, entering your name and mine so that the day will come when you and I repent and trust in Christ.

Believers sang this song for perhaps four or five centuries without any sign that it was true. And then, quite suddenly, in the twinkling of an eye in historical terms, Zion began to be visibly glorious. Calvin says, 'It is impossible to express in language adequate to the subject the glory with which Christ beautified his Church by his advent.' Quite suddenly, from the day of Pentecost onwards, men and women speaking different languages, inhabiting varied cultures, from all social classes, began to get citizenship in Zion, in the worldwide Church of Christ. And what a glorious Church it is, growing so fast in Africa, in South America, in parts of Asia. In China after seven decades of communism, there are more Christians than members of the communist party.

If we learn nothing else of Zion in the Psalms, we will do well to let the Psalms stir up and deepen in us this affection, remembering that it is an affection, first for Jesus Christ but then for the Church of Christ, which is the foreshadowing here on earth of all that Zion is promised to be. It is therefore an affection for the things of Christ, the things of Christ's gospel, and the things of Christ's church. As Jonathan Edwards wrote,

> Is there anything which Christians can find in heaven or earth so worthy to be the objects of their admiration and love, their earnest and longing desires, their hope, and their rejoicing, and their fervent zeal, as those things that are held forth to us in the gospel of Jesus Christ?[20]

---

20. Jonathan Edwards, *The Religious Affections*, [Banner 1961 (1st published 1746)].

The Psalms will stir in us the 'pure devotion' of the Church, Christ's Bride, for our Bridegroom (2 Cor. 11:3).

14. Exile in the Psalms

Psalm 2 affirms in the strongest possible terms that the LORD has determined that His King will rule the world from Zion, His holy mountain. We have seen that the two foundations of His rule are the King Himself and the Temple. While that Temple stands and the King in David's line reigns, the people had this strong confidence that all was well with the world, that their covenant religion was true, that whatever might happen in the world, these pillars would stand. It was – they thought – an unconditional guarantee of safety. After all, they might have said, even when the northern Kingdom of Israel was wiped off the map by the Assyrians, Jerusalem under King Hezekiah was saved (2 Kings 18,19). Everywhere else may be dangerous, but in Jerusalem we are safe.

Jeremiah, perhaps more than any other prophet, preached repeatedly that their confidence was a false assurance. In one dramatic gesture, God told Jeremiah to stand at the gate of the Temple and preach this message:

7 ¹ This is the word that came to Jeremiah from the LORD: ² 'Stand at the gate of the LORD's house and there proclaim this message:

"Hear the word of the LORD, all you people of Judah who come through these gates to worship the LORD. ³ This is what the LORD Almighty, the God of Israel, says: Reform your ways and your actions, and I will let you live in this place. ⁴ Do not trust in deceptive words and say, 'This is the temple of the LORD, the temple

of the LORD, the temple of the LORD!' ⁵ If you really change your ways and your actions and deal with each other justly, ⁶ if you do not oppress the foreigner, the fatherless or the widow and do not shed innocent blood in this place, and if you do not follow other gods to your own harm, ⁷ then I will let you live in this place, in the land I gave to your ancestors for ever and ever. ⁸ But look, you are trusting in deceptive words that are worthless."'
(Jer. 7:1-8)

The events described in 2 Kings 24 and 25, 2 Chronicles 36, and Jeremiah 52 were traumatic beyond our wildest nightmares. In one terrible stroke, the Babylonians ended the Davidic dynasty, destroyed the Temple, and took the people out of the Promised Land into Exile. These events would have been terrible in the normal course of human history; they were far worse for Israel. They did not just lose their government and their land; they lost the presence of God. What happened was that God 'thrust them from his presence' (Jer. 52:3). Geoffrey Grogan describes it like this:

> The most difficult experiences in life are those in which people face assaults on their basic convictions... This kind of experience is particularly distressing when these convictions relate to God. It is bad enough when just a single conviction about God is attacked, but when it is a whole web of convictions that has undergirded the life of a person or community, then something akin to despair is not far away, and despair is very serious, for in its ultimate form it is a function of atheism.[21]

The Babylonian Exile cast a long shadow over the Old Testament. When Matthew begins his gospel with a genealogy

---

21. Grogan 2008:274.

of the Messiah, his punctuation points are Abraham, with whom the covenant began; then, second, David, in whose reign that covenant reached its high point, changed into a higher key with the King ruling from the holy mountain, made holy by the Temple; but, third, 'the exile to Babylon' (see Matt. 1:1-17). This is one of the most significant events in Old Testament history. We see its mark especially in the writing of the books of Jeremiah, of 1 and 2 Samuel and 1 and 2 Kings, which conclude in exile (2 Kings 25:27-30), in the five poems of Lamentations, and in the Psalms.

Books 1 and 2 of the Psalter are mainly 'of David.' They conclude with a tremendous – even rousing – prayer for the worldwide rule of the King (Ps. 72), rounded off with an ascription of praise (Ps. 72:18-19) and a concluding note about 'the prayers of David son of Jesse' (v. 20). The contrast when we enter Book 3 would be hard to exaggerate; Book 3 smells of exile. It begins with Psalm 73, in which the Asaphite Psalmist laments the prosperity of the wicked and begins to doubt the promises of God. It ends with Psalm 89, which celebrates the unbreakable covenant with David (vv. 1-37) before concluding with agonised perplexity that this unbreakable covenant appears to be well and truly broken (vv. 38-51). In between these end markers there are some very explicit references to the Exile. Here are two examples:

> they burned your sanctuary to the ground (Ps. 74:7)

> O God, the nations have invaded your inheritance;
> they have defiled your holy temple,
> they have reduced Jerusalem to rubble (Ps. 79:1)

These clear references encourage us to read all of Book 3 with the Exile as the original background to the compilation of this section of the Psalter. It is not that every one of these Psalms was necessarily first composed during the Exile; after all, Psalm 86 is headed 'of David' and would seem to be an older, Davidic Psalm included here because of its appropriateness to the theme of Book 3. But there seems little doubt that the Babylonian Exile is the major theme of Book 3. This makes admirable sense of expressions of agonised perplexity. For example, when the Psalmist calls out, 'Will the Lord reject for ever? Will he never show his favour again?' (Ps. 77:7) or 'How long, LORD God Almighty, will your anger smoulder against the prayers of your people' (Ps. 80:4), it is natural to see the Exile as the event that has prompted these cries.

This is not to say that all the Psalms in Book 3 are only about the Exile, or that all the Psalms about the Exile only appear in Book 3. After all, the most famous such Psalm appears in Book 5 ('By the rivers of Babylon...' Ps. 137). In some ways, the theme is foreshadowed in the troubles of David that feature so large in Books 1 and 2; and it continues through Books 4 and 5. Whenever we read of God's wrath and judgment on His people, laments that they are 'scattered,' prayers for them to be 'gathered,' we do well to remember that the Exile is part of the broad background of thought.

With a risk of over-simplification, we may say that there are broadly three elements to the response of faith to the Exile: penitence, grieving, and claiming the covenant promises.

Penitence
The Exile was – paradoxically – a proof of the truth of Psalm 1. The wicked will not stand and their way does

lead to destruction. The God of Sinai had declared that covenant-breakers would be under a curse. That curse is spelled out in Deuteronomy 27 and 28 and affirmed in the Psalms (as we have seen in chapter 12).

The sinfulness of the people of God is reiterated in the historical review of Psalm 78, with phrases like these: '...a stubborn and rebellious generation, whose hearts were not loyal to God...they...refused to live by his law... But they continued to sin against him...God's anger rose against them...they kept on sinning...they did not believe...' Although those relate to the Exodus generation, their application to the generation of the Exile will have been obvious to all. The persistent sinfulness of Israel is acknowledged likewise in the prayer of Psalm 79:8: 'Do not hold against us the sins of past generations...'

Perhaps the strongest expression of explicit penitence comes in the final Psalm of Book 4. 'We have sinned, even as our ancestors did; we have done wrong and acted wickedly' (Ps. 106:6); this is followed by an account of the sinfulness of the Exodus generation, but explicitly linked to that of Israel in all generations. At the end of this Psalm they cry, 'Save us, LORD our God, and gather us from the nations...' (v. 47), which is precisely a prayer to be brought back from Exile.

There is implicit acknowledgment of sin also in Psalm 81. Here God laments that 'my people would not listen to me' (v. 11) looking back to the Exodus generation, but still appeals – in the present time – 'If my people would only listen to me...how quickly I would subdue their enemies...' (vv. 13, 14). So an admission that the Exile vindicated the God of Sinai is part of the response in the Psalms.

Grieving

As well as penitence for the persistent sin of Israel, we find expressed a deep grief at the dishonour brought to God by the destruction of the Temple and all that the Temple stood for. Psalm 74 pre-eminently helps us *feel* this grief. Verses 3-8 describe the pain, as we watch the Babylonians, like drunken vandals, trashing the most Holy Place on earth. This was 'the sanctuary' (v. 3), the place of God's holiness; it was 'where you met with us' (v. 4), the only place on earth where human beings could meet with God without being burned alive; it was 'the dwelling-place of your Name' (v. 7), where God was revealed and dwelt on earth.

And yet they cursed, scrawled obscene graffiti, urinated over it, trashed it with utter disregard for its holiness. We feel a strong and traumatic reaction when a home that is precious to us has been burgled and vandalised. As we see precious memories strewn over the floor, photographs smashed, letters torn and burned, our hearts grieve with shock and sadness. How much more ought we to feel the same when the dwelling-place of God on earth is treated like this! All through your childhood you had been told that behind that curtain was the Most Holy Place, where God dwelt on earth. You knew that only one man could enter that room, and only once a year, and only with sacrifice. But now you see godless Babylonians marching in there. It is a horrifying scene, and so deeply perplexing, as the Psalmist cries 'how long?' (v. 10). They cried that for half a millennium, until a mother placed her baby boy in the arms of an aged prayer-warrior, who had prayed often for 'the consolation of Israel,' and Simeon knew that his prayers were answered (Luke 2:25-32).

As this boy grew, He no doubt sang this Psalm and lamented the state of the people of God. He wept over Jerusalem (Luke 19:41-44), and then He Himself, the walking 'temple' of God on earth, was destroyed (John 2:19-22). As His disciples wept, perhaps they sang this Psalm, grieving the ugly, naked, blood-stained destruction of the most wonderful place on earth, where God Himself dwelt and walked. We too, even after His resurrection, grieve the desolate state of Christ's church as we watch God's enemies – both outside the church and within – trashing what should be a morally beautiful place. The persecuted and troubled church in every age has sung this Psalm, and we must sing it with them. We should never get used to the troubled state of Christ's church on earth; this Psalm helps us renew our grief.

Claiming the Covenant Promises

Alongside penitence and grief there runs a third – and essential – strand of response. One of the great puzzles of the whole Old Covenant era was how Psalms 1 and 2 could be true at the same time. If God is the God of Psalm 1, then the wickedness endemic to the people of God in all generations should guarantee that they – along with the rest of humanity – will be destroyed in the judgment. They are without God and without hope in the world (Eph. 2:12) just like everybody else. And yet Psalm 2 declares that a human King of Israel will rule the world. How can this be possible?

So the third strand expresses belief – albeit puzzled belief – that the promise of Psalm 2 is true. Indeed that all the promises of the covenant are true, that the God of the covenant really is faithful and His covenant love endures for ever (cf. Ps. 136). Given that God has made His promises, the Exile cannot be the end of the story. And so they cry out, 'How long?' rather than 'If only' or 'But now it's too late'.

How does the New Testament teach us to read the Exile?

The resolution of the paradox of Psalms 1 and 2 cannot come until all the promises of the covenant find their 'Yes' in Jesus Christ (2 Cor. 1:20). He is the righteous King of Psalm 1 who can therefore inherit the promises of Psalm 2. Furthermore, He is – in His own body – the Temple in which God places His feet on earth. When 'this temple' – His body – is destroyed, the sin of His people is paid for; when He 'rebuilds it in three days' their vindication is assured (John 2:19-22). And so, by His active obedience in life and supremely by His suffering and sin-bearing obedience in death, the many are made righteous (Rom. 5:19).

This explains why the final punctuation mark in Matthew's genealogy – after Abraham, David, and the Exile – is the birth of Jesus the Messiah (Matt. 1:1-17). He is the seed of Abraham (Gal. 3:16), the Son of David, and the end of Exile.

So part of the way in which we sing Psalms about the Exile is to grasp their fulfilment in and through the death of Jesus Christ. In the agony of the Exile we see a fore-shadowing of the sufferings of Christ. In the sin that caused the Exile we see that sin that Jesus bore for us. In the gathering of God's people at the end of Exile we see the destiny of Christ's Church.[22]

---

22. Ash 2010.

But there is another, and in some ways equally important, way in which we pray the Exile Psalms. We have seen (chapter 13) that the church of Jesus Christ, because it is the Body of Christ on earth and the place where God's Spirit dwells, is the Temple of the Holy Spirit. In the grief they experienced at the destruction of the Temple we feel the sadness as the grievous state of Christ's Church here on earth. And in the covenant promises to which they clung we have our own hope for the final rebuilding and perfection of the Church of Christ on earth.

15. Lament and Praise in the Psalms[23]

Paul wrote to the church in Philippi that he expected to continue his ministry, 'for your progress and joy in the faith' (Phil. 1:25). Those two words, 'progress' and 'joy' are worth considering. Progress in the faith is the objective maturing, in which believers and churches become more like Jesus. It is visible; Paul expects Timothy to grow in grace, 'so that everyone may *see* your progress' (1 Tim. 4:15). Joy is the subjective appropriation of the blessings of the gospel of Christ.[24] Paul prays for both. The Psalms likewise help us both to make progress (objectively) in Christ and to experience joy in Christ (subjectively). Praise and joy are intimately related.

C. S. Lewis famously wrote that 'praise almost seems to be inner health made audible.'[25] I remember once, when I was struggling in pastoral ministry, a friend made the

---

23. See James Hely Hutchinson, 'The Psalms and Praise' in Johnston and Firth 2005, chapter 4.

24. Bockmuehl 1997:94.

25. Lewis 1961:80.

mistake of asking me if I was enjoying my work; I more
or less bit his head off and said a firm 'no!' But afterwards,
as I reflected on my answer, albeit that it was true, I had
this unsettling feeling that if lack of joy became my default,
I would be in grave danger from siren voices luring me on to
the rocks. It is true that the inward experience of joy comes
and goes in the Christian life; but it is important that it
does not go away completely. The Psalms help us greatly
with this.

Overview of praise in the Psalms
In the Hebrew Old Testament the overall heading for
the Psalter is simply 'Praises' (*tehillim*). This is surprising,
because there is significantly more lament than praise in
the Psalter as a whole. So why is it not called 'laments (with
a few praises)'? The structure of the Psalter shows that
praise is a definitive facet of the Psalms. Each of the first
four Books ends with a clear ascription of praise (Ps. 41:13,
72:18-19, 89:52, and 106:48). This is particularly surprising
at the end of Psalm 89, since the final section of the Psalm
has been unmitigated perplexity and lament (vv. 38-51);
and then suddenly, apparently out of nowhere, 'Praise be to
the LORD for ever! Amen and Amen.'

What is more, there is a gradual crescendo of praise
as we near the end of Book 5. Psalms 111-118 include the
repeated refrain 'Hallelujah,' which is a plural exhortation,
'You (plural), praise the LORD!' (KJV 'Praise *ye* the
LORD!'). Perhaps this group, along with Psalm 119, at one
time formed the conclusion of the Psalter. We meet it again
in Psalm 135, and then in that great Hallelujah Chorus
from Psalm 146 to Psalm 150. So, although there are ups
and downs and there is much variety, the overall movement

of the Psalter is from lament towards praise. It is rather like the flight deck on the old aircraft carriers, tilted upwards at the end.

Why the transitions between lament and praise?

One important question in learning to pray the Psalms is the transitions between prayer or lament, and praise. Psalm 13 offers a simple example. In verses 1-4 David cries out in urgent prayer, punctuated by the agonised question 'how long?' But then, in verses 5 and 6, the tone changes to confidence and joy, ending with singing the LORD's praise. Scholars have suggested two unhelpful theories as to what lies behind these transitions.

The first is cultic; that is to say, if the context of the Psalm is Temple worship (as often seems likely), then perhaps a priest has come to the praying worshipper to give him or her some reassurance from God; after receiving this reassurance, the worshipper changes their tone from lament to praise. One problem with this is that there is no evidence in the rest of the Old Testament that this happened. Another – and really insuperable – problem is that the transitions not infrequently happen the other way around. For example, in Psalm 40, the first ten verses are marked by confidence, faith, and praise; but then, from verse 11 to the end, the tone changes to lament and urgent troubled prayer. In Psalm 31, to take another example, there is more than one transition; the Psalm oscillates between confident praise and agonised prayer. There is this two-way traffic between fear and faith. This raises the comical scenario that the Psalmist goes to the Temple cheerful and full of faith, but half way through their praise, a priest interrupts to lower their spirits with some oracle of doom! The cultic theory should be abandoned.

The second theory is that these transitions reflect, not anything in the actual prayers or praises of worshippers, but rather the 'cut and paste' work of literary editors, who spent their lives stitching together otherwise unrelated pieces of piety, a lament stitched on to a hymn of praise, and so on. This too is unpersuasive.

No, the transitions – in both directions – are entirely explicable in terms of the dynamics of the life of faith. We know in our own experience that sadness and perplexity may change to a glad confidence in the gospel, but also that strong confidence may give way again to urgent and sorrowful prayer. Martin Luther used to describe the strong experience of deep grappling with God as *Anfechtung*. Writing from prison, Dietrich Bonhoeffer movingly wrote about this:

> I have never realized so clearly what the Bible and Luther mean by spiritual trial [Anfechtung]. Quite suddenly, for no apparent reason, whether physical or psychological, the peace and placidity which have been a mainstay hitherto begin to waver, and the heart ... becomes that defiant and despondent thing one cannot fathom. It is like an invasion from outside, as though evil powers were trying to deprive one of life's dearest treasures.[26]

How often, in the midst either of personal Bible reading and prayer, or a church gathering, our hearts have been filled with praise in the one moment, and in the next assailed by temptations to self-pity, lust, anxiety, resentment, envy, bitterness, or just a cloying coldness of heart. And then again by gospel confidence. What a strange thing is the human heart! The Psalms understand and express this with perfect realism.

---

26. Bonhoeffer 1960:32,33 quoted in Anderson 1970:75,76.

How do we get from prayer to praise?

In his magisterial study, *Praise and Lament in the Psalms*, Claus Westermann observes that, almost without exception 'there is no, or almost no, such thing as "mere" lament and petition.' He deduces that, 'The cry to God is here never one-dimensional, without tension' (i.e. just lament and petition). Rather, 'It is always somewhere in the middle between petition and praise. By nature it cannot be *mere* petition or lament, but is *always underway from supplication to praise.*'[27] It is worth considering why. Lament is the natural human response to sorrow and pain. We grieve, we mourn, we weep. There is nothing special about that; it is common human experience.

But – and this is a very big difference – the moment we address our lament upwards in prayer to the true God, the God and Father of Jesus Christ, and that prayer is heard in heaven, it becomes something more than the outpouring of human sorrow. It contains within itself, by the ministry of the Spirit of God who groans in and through our prayers, the seeds of a future rescue and therefore of praise. Praise is the appropriation in the present of truths that will only be consummated in the future. We praise, not because the present is easy, but because the future is glorious. Praise is therefore not the outpouring of hearts made glad by present happy circumstances, but the expression of faith in hearts made glad, in the midst of suffering, by the assurance of future glory.

The normal context for prayer and praise is the Assembly of the People of God led by their King

At this point we come back to the paradigm of the Assembly or Congregation of the People of God led by the King in

---

27. Westermann 1981:75 (my italics).

prayers and praises to God in heaven. This context makes sense of two frequent phenomena in the Psalms, the otherwise strange switches from singular to plural, and also the unselfconscious switches from third person speech (declaring the praises of God to one another) to and from second person speech (telling God how praise-worthy He is). For example,

> 3rd   Great is the LORD in Zion
>   *he* is exalted over all the nations.
>
> 2nd   Let them praise *your* great and glorious name –
> 3rd   *he* is holy.
>
> 3rd   The King is mighty, *he* loves justice –
> 2nd   *you* have established equity;
>   in Jacob *you* have done
>   what is just and right.
>
> 3rd   Exalt the LORD our God
>   and worship at his footstool;
>   he is holy.
>   (Ps. 99:2-5)[28]

Notice how the voice switches to and fro between the address to the assembled congregation and speaking to God Himself. It is as if the Leader of the Congregation moves his eyes from a horizontal gaze round the Assembly whom he leads, upwards to the God whom he worships, and then back again. The Church of God is in the presence of God, led by their praise-leader, who is their King.

---

28. Hely Hutchison cites Psalm 93 and Psalm 118:21-25 as other examples.

The Psalms encourage praise that is meditative as well as declaratory[29]

It is possible for praise simply to declare, and sing with confidence, some great truth about God. But authentic praise will sometimes – perhaps more often – arise from thoughtful, sometimes troubled, meditation on the ways in which circumstances seem to contradict these truths. Our hearts need to be meditative, to think carefully, before they can pour themselves out in voices that are declaratory. 'The Psalms are designed to help people who don't always feel like praising begin by meditating on the mess the world is in, and only through a full and robust process of meditation, to come out with praise.'[30] Psalm 150 comes at the end, not at the beginning, of the Psalter! By contrast, the songs in heaven are 'new' not because their content is new, but because they will have no more wrestling or perplexity mixed in with them.[31]

This means that when praying the Psalms of praise, we must not divorce them – in our prayers or in our popular Christian songs loosely based on the Psalms – from the perplexity and faith-filled reasoning that informs and finally issues in the praise.

Praise clears our heads and hearts

In his rather mixed but sometimes insightful work, *Israel's Praise*, Walter Brueggemann has a section in which he describes praise as 'a Constitutive Act'. By this he means that when we make the praises of God a regular part of our life together as believers, it will shape our worldview.

---

29. See Lefebvre 2010, chapter 5.

30. Lefebvre 2010:97.

31. Lefebvre 2010:134f.

It is the act of praise, the corporate, regularized, intentional, verbalized, and enacted act of praise, through which
the community of faith creates, orders, shapes, imagines,
and patterns the world of God, the world of faith, the
world of life, in which we are to act in joy and obedience.[32]

This is both helpful and dangerous at the same time. It
is dangerous if by it we understand that our praises can
actually *create* a particular kind of world by our imagination
and declaration. For the world exists and the God we praise
exists objectively and really, in a way that cannot be changed
by our praises. But it is helpful insofar as it recognises that
there are all sorts of other thought-worlds being created
around us by advertising, the media, propaganda, cultural
norms, and so on. Brueggemann calls praise 'the act of
world-formation'; it is rather the act of shaping our hearts
and convictions by the true world that God has already
formed. But Brueggemann is right that by our praises
we 'delegitimise' other thought-worlds: 'The church sings
praises not only toward God but against the gods.'[33]

To join in the congregational praise of God in the Psalms
is a deeply significant practice. In what Brueggemann
calls 'the geography of imagination' we call our hearts
out of 'Babylon' and back to God's city. These Psalms are
'dangerous poems' – dangerous, that is, to the gods of
Babylon, against whose empire these poems 'constitute
the greatest threat' because they shape us to disbelieve the
claims of Babylon and belong in our affections and our
convictions in the city of God.[34]

---

32. Brueggemann 2010:25f.

33. Brueggemann 2010:27.

34. Brueggemann 2010:50f.

Jesus Christ is our worship-leader and praise-leader

One of the most insightful and profoundly Christian comments I have read of the praises in the Psalms comes from Claus Westermann. It is worth quoting him at some length.

> The praise of the Old Testament remains in its center…a praise of expectation. It is 'a waiting' praise.

> We may surmise that the imperative call to praise in the late Psalms is given such great prominence because behind it there is hidden anxiety, whether God will really be praised enough, whether he will be praised aright.

> This imperative call to praise…served in its very preponderance as a sign that in this people *all voices called for a praise that was yet to be given.* This imperative too awaited the fulfilling of praise.

> The expectation of the Old Testament is fulfilled in Jesus Christ. So must also the 'praise in expectation' be fulfilled in him. The Gospel according to John says…that Christ is come to 'honor' the Father among men. This *doxazein* can also be translated as 'praise.'

> Christ is come to honor the Father in his life and in his death. At the turning point of his life stands the word, John 17:1, 'Father,…glorify thy Son that the Son may glorify [=praise] thee.' Verse 26, 'I made known to them thy name, and I will make it known.' cf. Ps. 22:22, 'I will tell of thy name to my brethren.' This is the intent of the vow of praise of the Psalms. In the Prologue the work of Jesus Christ is summed up in 'The only Son, who is in the bosom of the Father, he has made him known.' *He has done that which it was the intention of the praise of the people of Israel to do.*[35]

---

35. Westermann 1981:161 (my italics).

Writing of that same quotation of Psalm 22:22 in Hebrews 2:12, Philip Ryken writes,

> These words – that is, 'I will declare your name to my brothers and sisters; in the assembly I will sing your praise' – refer to the worship that Jesus offered at the temple and the synagogue. Envision the Son of God singing the Psalms the Spirit inspired and using them to praise the Father. By faith in Christ, that perfect worship now belongs to us, as if we ourselves had offered it to God. This is part of what it means for us to know Christ: our imperfect worship is accepted by the Father because of the perfect worship offered by the Son.[36]

To understand how this revolutionises the way we praise God, I will illustrate from the first two verses of Psalm 145.

Jesus the praise-leader in Psalm 145

> A Psalm of praise. Of David.
>
> [1] I will exalt you, my God the King;
>   I will praise your name for ever and ever.
> [2] Every day I will praise you
>   and extol your name for ever and ever.
>   (Ps. 145:1-2)

Here is what happens when we draw a straight line from the 'I' of the Psalm to the 'I' that is me. You might think of this as an outtake from the beginning of a bad sermon on the Psalm. It runs something like this.

> This Psalm begins with three words for praise, translated in NIV 'exalt,' 'praise,' and 'extol.' They mean much the same thing; but together they speak of a praise that is

---

36. Ryken 2010:122.

unreserved. It is praise from all of the mind, all the heart, all the emotions, all the affections, the whole body, all of me. So let me ask: is your praise of God unreserved? Is every corner of your being given over unreservedly to the praise of God, holding nothing back? Or do you hold back, perhaps with a part of your thinking, or with mixed motives, or ambiguous affections and desires? I suspect that you do (you wicked person).

What is more, it speaks of a praise that is *unbroken.* I praise 'every day'. There are no breaks, no days off praising, no bad praise days. So what about you? Is your praise of God unbroken? Or do you sometimes have time off from praising? I am guessing you do (you wicked person).

And, not only is this praise unreserved and unbroken, it is also *unending.* It goes on 'for ever and ever.' It never fades. So, again, I need to ask you: will your praise be unending? Or will it fade away? I fear that it will (you wicked person).

I have exaggerated to make a point. But that would be a terrible start to a sermon, just beating people over the head with the knowledge of what failures they are in praise. It invites one of three unsatisfactory responses. Some – if they are very shallow – will nod their heads and say an unreserved and self-righteous 'yes' to all those challenges. 'Yes, my praise of God is pretty much unreserved, unbroken, and unending. Well done, me.' That is hypocrisy. Others will put up their hands and say, 'No, you've got me there. I don't do this as I ought. But I know that I ought to. And I am going to try so so much harder to do this in the days to come. I will add "remember to praise God" as a perpetual reminder on my phone; I will try very very hard to do better.' Such zealotry may be admirable, but is doomed to failure. So a third group will simply despair: 'I knew I was a sinner and failed in so many ways. Now I must add to that my failure in praise. I always thought I was a loser, and now I know I am.' None of those responses is a gospel response, because that reading of verses 1 and 2 is not a gospel reading.

Sadly, that kind of energetic and zealous exhortation to praise is not uncommon. I remember visiting to preach in a church in another country, and the meeting began with forty-five minutes of utterly mindless exhortations to try harder to praise God better; after that I felt more miserable than ever, because it was as if I had been beaten over the head. Mere exhortation to praise will not, and cannot, turn our hearts to praise, because there is no gospel in it.

So what will turn our hearts to praise? This is very important, for the theological reason that if God is not praised, then God is not made known. God is immeasurably great, and therefore to know Him is to praise Him. Not to praise Him is not to know Him. Praise is not the icing on the Christianity cake; it is the necessary condition of the true God being made known.

It is the gospel – and only the gospel – that will turn our hearts to praise. And the gospel, in this respect, is the news that Jesus Christ is our praise leader. We discover this by a careful reading of these two verses to see what they actually say, and who is speaking to whom. This is a Psalm of David, who is the human King; and he addresses his praises to 'God the King.' So the (human) King praises God the King. As the representative head of the people of God, the King pledges unreserved, unbroken, and unending praise to God the King in heaven.

The problem is that David did not do what he pledged to do. Praise means two things: it means telling someone how good, beautiful, talented, or virtuous, they are; and it means telling other people how good, beautiful, talented, or virtuous, this person is. I can praise my lovely wife to her face, telling her how lovely she is (and I do); and I can praise her to others, telling you (my readers) how lovely my wife is. In a similar way, no doubt David told the LORD God in his spoken or sung praises how great and good He is. That would have been a good and natural thing to do. We can do the same. It is not too difficult to sing songs of praise to God, or to praise Him in our prayers, and to mean it. But the other dimension of praise – telling and showing others how great and good God is – may not be so easy. It means that David has pledged, with his life and his lips, to bear consistent witness to the goodness and greatness of the LORD God. To bring glory to God by his life and his lips, unreservedly, unbrokenly, and unendingly. Very sadly, David did not do that; his adultery with Bathsheba and all the sinful cover-up that followed is only the worst example of his failures. Besides, the day came when he died, so his praise could not go on 'for ever and ever.'

David – and we have seen this time and again in the Psalms – is speaking by the Spirit of Christ, and calling 'for a praise that was yet to be given.' All down Old Testament history these voices called on the King, and on the people, to praise the LORD God unreservedly, unbrokenly, and unendingly. And no one did. No king did that, no priest, no governor, no Sadduccee, no Pharisee, no one. Until – about a thousand years after David – a boy sang the Psalms in synagogue. And as He grew – a child, a youth, a young man – every time He heard the call to praise in the Psalms it met with an answering cry from His own heart: 'Yes, yes, yes, I will do that. I will exalt you, my God the King; I will praise your name for ever and ever. Every day I will praise you and extol your name for ever and ever. I will.' And He did. With every word of His lips, each action of His life, and every affection of His heart He gave glory to the Father and proclaimed how great He was. With consistency, with integrity, with perseverance, with perfection, He made the Father known. As in Psalm 22, where David says, 'I will declare your name to my people; in the assembly I will praise you,' so here, Jesus does what David prophesied (Heb. 2:12). The words that were David's in shadow became Jesus's in substance. In the praises of David we hear the praises of Jesus Christ. He is the King who praises the King, the one who, at the end of His life, can say, 'Father...I have brought you glory on earth' (John 17:4). In making the Father perfectly known, Jesus did that which the praises of Israel were meant to do.

And then, at the end of this Psalm, the King sings,

> My mouth will speak in praise of the LORD.
> Let every creature praise his holy name
>   for ever and ever. (v. 21)

This is where we come in. Every creature is invited to praise God as we are led by our King. In some ways Psalms 146–150, the great Hallelujah Chorus that concludes the Psalms, is the response to this call.

It is a great encouragement to us, in our many failures, our down days, our sin, and our lack of praise, to grasp that these exhortations to praise are not a challenge to take the microphone at the front of the stage, but an invitation to join the choir headed by Jesus our praise-leader. When I worked for the Proclamation Trust, one of my colleagues used to sit in a restrained conservative sort of way at her desk during the day (we were that kind of organisation); but then she would slip away and – if pressed – shyly admit that she was going to be a backing singer for stars like Jamelia, Take That, or Emeli Sandé. She was our connection with cool. In a way, that is what it is to be a Christian – not to be the lead singer, for that position is taken, but to be part of the backing group. The praises of the Psalms are the praises of Jesus and we join Him in singing them.

One of our Cornhill students started a Mexican Wave. He and three friends wondered how these wonderful waves got started, and resolved to try. They were at Wembley Stadium watching an England football game against Croatia. At a suitable moment the four of them stood and went 'whoa!' No one paid any attention, and they sat down feeling rather silly. A little later they tried again; about thirty people joined in but then it fizzled out. But on the third attempt, it took off and went right round that huge stadium. All round the stadium thousands of individual decisions had to be made. Do I stand when the wave reaches me, or do I stay rooted to my seat? That is a light-hearted illustration to make a point. When the great wave of the people of God's praise of God reaches me, my decision is not whether or not to initiate the praise; for that has already been done by Jesus. My decision is whether or not to join in the praise that Jesus has already started, and which Jesus will lead for eternity, the King praising the King. This is gospel. It is miserable moralism and law simply to exhort me to praise God in my own energy and by my own rights; I cannot and will not do it. It is wonderful gospel to tell me of a Saviour who praises the Father and makes Him perfectly known, and who invites me to join His choir. That is the joy of the Christian life.

Part Four:

HOW TO TEACH THE PSALMS

In this final section of volume 1 we consider what it will mean to teach or preach the Psalms in such a way that we and all who hear us will learn to sing and pray the Psalms for ourselves.

16. How Hebrew poetry works

We begin this part with a more technical chapter. But I hope I have made it accessible to the non-specialist, and specifically to the majority who are not able to read the Psalms in Hebrew. When you are reading – and seeking to pray – the Psalms, you are reading an English translation of poetry written in Hebrew. It is a help to have some idea of how this poetry 'works'.

Hebrew poetry doesn't rhyme

Even when you read it in Hebrew, the lines don't rhyme. This is a good thing, as rhyme is notoriously difficult to carry over into translation. There are sometimes plays on how words sound, and a good commentary will alert you to these. But these are of relatively small importance.

Hebrew poetry has rhythm, although this is harder to detect in translation

Although it does not rhyme, it does usually have a meter. That is to say, there is – in the original – some rhythm, which would have made it easier to speak out loud and remember. The two most common rhythms are 3:3 and 3:2.

For an example of 3:3 rhythm, take Psalm 26:2. The stress in the two lines would be read like this:

> Test me, LORD, and try me,
> Examine my heart and my mind.

Laments often use a 3:2 meter, where the falling cadence (from 3 to 2) may suggest sadness, or sometimes a quiet confidence as, for example, in Psalm 27:1:

> The LORD is my light and my salvation –
> whom shall I fear?

However, it is difficult to know the meter from an English translation, and probably it doesn't matter too much.

In Hebrew poetry, mood and meaning are conveyed mainly through parallelism

The most obvious feature of Hebrew poetry, even in translation, is that it comes in relatively short lines rather than continuous text. The most significant vehicle that Hebrew poetry employs to convey both mood and meaning is parallelism, the relationships between these lines.

In a popular song called 'There are nine million bicycles in Beijing', the singer Katie Melua illustrated how parallelism can work. Here are three different examples:

(a) There are nine million bicycles in Beijing; that's a
    fact. It's a thing we can't deny
(b) like the fact that I will love you till I die.

Here the parallelism is direct: one fact (a) parallels another
fact (b).

(a) We are twelve billion light years from the edge;
     that's a guess, no-one can ever say it's true;
(b) but I know that I will always be with you.

Here the parallelism works by contrast: the first line (a) is
an uncertain guess, the second (b) is a sure truth.

(a) There are six billion people on the earth, more or
     less; and it makes me feel quite small;
(b) but you're the one I love the most of all.

Here the second line builds on the first line to intensify the
truth it declares.

Most Hebrew poetry comes in bicola, the technical
term for two parallel lines. More rarely, there may be
tricola, three parallel lines. There is considerable variety in
the ways the parallel lines develop meaning.

Synonymous Parallelism

In the simplest kind (sometimes called synonymous
parallelism) the two lines say essentially the same thing in
slightly different ways. Here is a very simple example:

(a) No one who practises deceit will dwell in my house;
(b) no one who speaks falsely will stand in my presence.
     (Ps. 101:7)

The two lines are almost identical, but just use slightly
different words or phrases. The effect is to emphasise the
truth by repetition.

More often in so-called synonymous parallelism, there is some slight development or intensification. For example,

(a) See how your enemies growl,
(b) how your foes rear their heads. (Ps. 83:2)

The intensification comes in the last part of each line. First (a) they 'growl' indicating their hostility; but then (b) they 'rear their heads,' an idiom indicating actual rebellion.

Here is a three-line example to show intensification:

(a) I remember the days of long ago;
(b) I meditate on all your works
(c) and consider what your hands have done
        (Ps. 143:5).

The words 'remember,' 'meditate on,' and 'consider' are synonymous. They press home the thoughtful activity of the Psalmist. But notice how the second part of each line develops in intensity. In (a) he remembers time past, in a rather general sense. Then in (b) he makes it clear that the past time he remembers is, more precisely, 'your works,' what the LORD has done. But then (c) makes it very personal and immediate: 'what your *hands* have done.' At one level the three lines convey the same truth; at another they build that truth in a crescendo of intensity.

Antithetical Parallelism

At the opposite end of the spectrum is parallelism in which the lines express the positive and negative sides of a truth. This is sometimes called antithetic parallelism. For example,

(a) For the LORD watches over the way of the
        righteous,
(b) but the way of the wicked leads to destruction.
        (Ps. 1:6)

(b) is the flip side of (a). The effect is to press the truth home to us both positively (for encouragement) and negatively (for warning).

Other kinds of Parallelism

Sometimes parallelism doesn't fit neatly into either the synonymous or antithetic categories. (b) may significantly develop the thought of (a), as in,

> (a) For great is your love towards me;
> (b) you have delivered me from the depths, from the realm of the dead. (Ps. 86:13)[1]

(a) makes a general affirmation about the LORD's covenant love; (b) makes this concrete in a particular rescue from death.

Or (b) may, as it were, ascend from (a), bringing (a) to its completion, as in,

> (a) For the LORD is the great God,
> (b) the great King above all gods. (Ps. 95:3)

The general statement of (a), that the covenant God of Israel (the LORD) is the 'great God' reaches its climax in (b): He is the King above every other so-called 'god'.

Staircase Parallelism

Especially in the Psalms of Ascent, we meet what is called 'Staircase parallelism,' in which the phrases gradually 'ascend' a staircase of meaning. Here is one example:

> I lift up my eyes to the mountains –
> where does my **help** come from?
>
> My **help** comes from the LORD,
> the Maker of heaven and earth.

---

1. This is a bicola (*pace* NIV format).

> He will not let your foot slip –
> **he who watches over** you will not **slumber**;
>> indeed, **he who watches over** Israel
>> will neither **slumber** nor sleep.
>>> (Ps. 121:1-4)

Notice how the meaning builds and how the repetitions of 'help,' 'he who watches over' and 'slumber' help convey the ascending meaning.

What to do with Parallelism

It is important not to skim over the parallelism. Some of us may feel the Psalm would have been more efficient if we had roughly halved the number of lines. We could have saved paper and conveyed the same cognitive content! But we would have lost much of the emotional and affectional impact of the Psalm. Let the parallel lines impact you; and let them make you think about the relationships between the lines. Hearing poetry is a little like viewing a distant object through binoculars rather than a telescope. Both eyes are engaged in binocular vision; the two views are very slightly different and their convergence produces a sense of depth.

Geoffrey Grogan writes of how the famous cultural commentator Marshall McLuhan distinguished between what he called 'hot' media and 'cool' media. A 'hot' medium is something like Television, which stimulates both eye and ear intensively and leaves little space for our imaginative engagement. But a 'cool' medium, like Radio, precisely because it 'presents an incomplete pattern of stimuli… requires a greater level of engagement on the part of the reader…Hebrew poetry is more like radio!' Read and hear the parallelism attentively, both thinking how it conveys meaning and feeling how it conveys mood.

As in other poetry, there tends to be a density of expression

Poetry tends to express its content and mood in few words. It is not usually expansive. To take a secular example, T.S.Eliot's poem *The Waste Land* begins like this:

> A crowd flowed over London Bridge
> so many, I had not thought death had undone
>   so many.

It is terse and cryptic. We are not told who these 'many' are, why they flow 'over London Bridge' or in what sense death has undone them.

To take a biblical example, in 1 Samuel 2, Hannah sings,

> The LORD brings death and makes alive;
> he brings down to the grave and raises up (v. 6).

We are not told whom He brings down to the grave, whom He raises up, or why. It is compressed.

Further, there is in the Psalms a deliberate imprecision. With a few exceptions, such as where the superscription gives us an indication (e.g. Ps. 34 'Of David. When he pretended to be insane before Abimelek, who drove him away and he left') or the content of the Psalm gives a clear clue (Ps. 137 'By the rivers of Babylon we sat and wept…'), we cannot locate a particular Psalm in biblical history. References to enemies, threats, illnesses, and victories are imprecise. This is deliberate and enables the Psalm to be appropriated by the people of God in many other circumstances.

This is even true, for example, of Hannah's song in 1 Samuel 2, where we know the exact circumstances that prompted the prayer. And yet the content of the prayer is so general that it can readily be sung by the people of God in other places and at other times.

Hebrew poetry makes much use of imagery
The Psalms are thick with imagery. In Psalm 1 there is a tree, and chaff. In Psalm 2 there is a rod of iron and a piece of pottery being smashed. In Psalm 80 Israel is compared to a fruitful vine. Do not skim over the imagery, but let it have its desired effect, not only on your mind but also on your emotions. Let the Psalms enrich your imagination. Feel a godly delight, fear, horror, hope, or whatever is appropriate, as the imagery indicates.

In Hebrew poetry there are many echoes of other Old Testament scriptures and there are future echoes in New Testament scriptures
The technical word for this is 'intertextuality,' how Bible texts bounce off one another and interpret one another. For example Psalm 104 derives much of its imagery from Genesis 1. As we read Psalm 104 we ought to hold in our minds God who spoke light, dry land and sea creatures into existence, and who divided the waters from the waters so that there could be habitable earth.

Poetry – perhaps more than prose – works by connotation as well as by denotation. It is not enough to ask what a particular word or phrase denotes (what it means, at the simplest level); we must also ask what company it keeps, what associations are called up in the minds and hearts of biblically literate hearers. For example, the moment you say 'the horse and his rider' to a thoughtful Bible reader, he or she immediately thinks of the Exodus; their mind and heart are there by the Red Sea, feeling the fear as the most powerful war machines on earth threatened them with annihilation, and the exhilarating praise that accompanied seeing 'the horse and his rider...cast into the sea' (Exod. 15:1).

One of the most common and emotive images in the Psalms is of flood waters, the waves and threat of the deep sea. In chapter 9 we saw how this imagery works, both cognitively (in what it conveys to our minds) and affectively (how it shapes our emotions, fears, and yearnings).

Try to get to know the Bible so well that you instinctively pick up more and more of these echoes. While you are getting to know the Bible better, a good commentary should draw your attention to the principal echoes elsewhere in the Old Testament, and also looking ahead to the New.

The translation of tenses in Hebrew poetry is uncertain
There are only two *forms* of Hebrew verb, the Perfect and the Imperfect. It is easy to know which *form* a verb takes; but in Hebrew poetry it is much less easy to translate that form into English tenses that indicate past, present, or future time. You can see this uncertainty by comparing some good English translations. Take, for example, Psalm 119:85a:

> NIV   The arrogant **dig** pits to trap me...
>
> NRSV The arrogant **have dug** pitfalls for me...
>
> ESV   The insolent **have dug** pitfalls for me...

The dominant theory used to be that Hebrew tenses were indicators of time

- The Hebrew Imperfect indicated present or future time.

- The Hebrew Perfect referred to past time.

More recently, scholars have tended to think that Hebrew tenses indicate *aspect*, which means whether an action is completed or uncompleted.

- The Hebrew Imperfect refers to uncompleted action; this will usually be present (ongoing) or future (not yet commenced), but may also be past (what we would call the past continuous).

- The Hebrew Perfect indicates a completed action; this is usually in the past but may be in the present or future (what we would call a future perfect tense).

William Craigie concludes, 'It is my view that not enough is yet known about the nature and development of the Hebrew verbal system to permit a sure translation of Hebrew verbs *in poetic texts* with respect to tense on the basis of the form alone.'[2]

So do not put too much store by the tense given in your translation. If in doubt, compare a couple of good translations to see if there is uncertainty.

No-one knows the meaning of 'Selah' in the Psalms

Seventy-one times in the Psalms, and three times in the Psalm of Habakkuk, the word 'Selah' appears. Mostly it appears in Psalms with superscriptions, and commonly ones that seem to indicate some musical connection (e.g. 'to the musical director' or 'to the choirmaster'). This may indicate some musical significance; we cannot be sure.

Sometimes 'Selah' appears at the end of an obvious section. For example, in Psalm 3:2 at the end of the first

2. Craigie 1983:110-113.

couplet, and then at the end of verse 4 after the second couplet, and finally at the end of verse 8, the conclusion of the Psalm. This might suggest that it was a division between sections, in terms of the meaning. Except that it sometimes occurs right in the middle of a section. For example, Psalm 68 verses 7 and 8 have 'Selah' in the middle as follows:

> When you, God, went out before your people,
> when you marched through the wilderness *Selah*
> the earth shook, the heavens poured down rain…

Guesses abound as to what 'Selah' means. But nobody knows. The NIV now omits the word from the main text and includes it in a footnote; other translations include it. Since we have no idea what it means, it probably doesn't matter very much.

17. The fourfold task of the Psalms Teacher

Praying the Psalms and preaching the Psalms are intimately connected. Only the one who prays the Psalms can hope fruitfully to teach the Psalms.

Teaching a Psalm is analogous to a music teacher training a pupil to sing a song. There are four elements in the process.

The Cognitive Dimension: understand the Lyrics

We need to do analysis. You can sing a song in a foreign language with no understanding, but you will not sing it well. Your teacher should take you through the words, explaining their meaning and force. We need to explain what the words and idioms mean, how they translate in biblical theology from their Old Covenant context into New

Covenant application today, and how they find fulfilment in Christ. Much of this handbook has focussed on this.

The Affective Dimension: feel the Tune

Analysis is necessary. But analysis is not enough. Reading and praying the Psalms is more than an exercise in scholarly dissection. We are music teachers, not biology teachers. A biology teacher may instruct in dissection, so that an organism is expertly cut into its constituent parts. But, as it is said, 'we murder to dissect'; a Psalm that is analysed and no more will die on the lips. We need – to continue the musical analogy – to teach the tune. Psalms are for the music room not the mortuary. By this I do not necessarily mean a literal setting to music, desirable though this may be. I leave that to those musicians who are capable of doing this well, and thank God for them. I mean 'tune' in the metaphorical sense of grasping and feeling the affectional dimensions of the Psalm. What desires, delights, fears, sorrows, and affections are being expressed? The Psalms are thick with emotions; we must not flatten them, make them grey or bland, but rather experience them with all their churnings.

A nineteenth-century commentator wrote that,

> No single book of Scripture, not even of the New Testament, has, perhaps, ever taken such a hold on the *heart* of Christendom. None, if we may dare judge, unless it be the Gospels, has had so large an influence in *moulding the affections*...of believers.[3]

The Psalms express relational intimacy with God, who is 'my God' or 'our God', whose 'eyes' are on all who fear Him

---

3. Perowne (1898) Vol. 1, p. 22. I am grateful to John F. Evans for this quotation. The italics are mine.

(Psalm 33:18), who is the subject of unfailing love and the
object of responsive love and longing.

The problem with some of us is that we are like Harris
in Jerome K. Jerome's classic, and quintessentially English,
comedy *Three Men in a Boat*. Three eccentric men in Edwar-
dian England decide to go on a riverboat holiday (with
Montmorency the dog). As they plan for the holiday, they
discuss whether to camp out at night or to stay in an inn.
'George and I,' writes the narrator, 'were for camping out. We
said it would be so wild and free, so patriarchal like.' There
follows an effusive and lengthy eulogy about the romance
of camping. And then, 'Harris said: "How about when it
rained?"' And the narrator comments, 'You can never rouse
Harris. There is no poetry about Harris – no wild yearning
for the unattainable. Harris never "weeps, he knows not why".
If Harris's eyes fill with tears, you can bet it is because Harris
has been eating raw onions, or has put too much Worcester
[sauce] over his chop.' There is no poetry about Harris. He
can cope with the cognitive and intellectual dimensions of
life; but he has stunted affections and emotions.

Poetry is given us precisely to deepen our affections and
enrich our emotions. It is a blend of the affective (touch-
ing our feelings) and the cognitive (addressing our minds),
in which the affective is commonly stronger than in prose.
Poetry does not communicate in the same way as does prose.
J. I. Packer has said that poems communicate not just 'from
head to head' but 'from heart to heart'. We should not press
this too far, as prose too has affective dimensions. But those
dimensions are stronger and more intense in poetry.

It is no accident that so much of the Bible is in poetry.
A student said to me, 'I think I am a Harris.' To which we
need to reply, 'God has chosen to give much of his revelation

to us in poetry. And we need to learn, not only to read it, but to feel it.'

It is said that the poet A. E. Housman did not dare to think of a line of poetry while shaving for fear that he would cut himself (in an age of cut-throat razors!).[4] He would be so moved that his heart would beat faster, his hands shake, and tears well up in his eyes. It may be a while before you respond to poetry with such intensity. But take your first steps. For the Psalms are 'prayed poetry.'[5] Our task is the lifelong project of so immersing ourselves in these poems that our minds and hearts are gripped.

Reading aloud is an important part of this, for the sound of the words is an integral part of the meaning, and that sound is only heard when read aloud. The fantasy novelist Philip Pullman writes, 'The sound is part of the meaning, and that part only comes alive when you speak it.' Pullman goes on to complain that 'I have come across teachers and student teachers whose job was to teach poetry, but who thought that poetry was only a fancy way of dressing up simple statements to make them look complicated, and that their task was to help their pupils translate the stuff into ordinary English…It has the effect of turning the classroom into a torture-chamber, in which everything that made the poem a living thing had been killed and butchered.'[6] Pullman is no believer, but he is right about poetry!

When a poem is summarised, much is lost, for it is in the totality of the spoken poem that it conveys its message.

---

4. Quoted by Philip Pullman in *The Daily Telegraph* 3rd Sept. 2005 p. 19.

5. Claus Westermann, quoted in Anderson 1970:21.

6. Philip Pullman, *The Daily Telegraph* 3rd Sept. 2005 p. 19.

We need to let a poem get to work on us, so to immerse ourselves in it that it gets in through every pore of our bodies and souls, right into our hearts.

The blend of the cognitive and the affective helps to answer the question: what should it *feel* like to be a Christian? What is authentic Christian experience? This is important for assurance, lest my disordered feelings lead me to doubt the reality of my salvation. It is significant for realistic expectations of what the Christian life will be like, so that we do not give up when the going gets tough. It matters for evangelism, so that we paint an honest picture of the life of discipleship into which we invite others to come. It has consequences for the stability of our walk with God; for if we do not have a true and rounded biblical view, we will be vulnerable to the siren voices calling us on to some other path – that if only we read this book, went on that course, attended the other conference, then we would get the first-class Christian life – but actually seducing us on to the rocks.

The Commitment Dimension: grasp the Significance

Before I join in, I should ask myself what it will mean for me to do so. That is, what is the significance of the song for me? It had some significance for the first singer; they sang it for a reason, to express some conviction, grief, confidence or joy. But what would it mean for me to add my voice to the choir?

Sometimes we listen to a song; at other times we join in. This is true of secular songs. Many of my generation listened to the Beatles: 'Yesterday, all my troubles seemed so far away; now it looks as if they're here to stay. O, I believe in yesterday...' Sometimes we sang along just because we liked the tune; but sometimes our joining in expressed some fellow-feeling with the one disappointed in love. Or when Bob Dylan sang in his nasal voice, 'Come gather round people wherever you roam and admit that the waters around you have grown…for the times they are a'changin'.' Some of us joined in because we identified with this song of 1960s' revolution and hailed the bright new world of freedom from repressed bourgeois restrictions. It wasn't a very good revolution, as we now know, but we were fooled, and that's why we joined in.

Singing the blues is done with greater conviction when I am feeling blue; otherwise my singing is just pretending. To sing 'Swing low, sweet chariot…' at Twickenham indicates – at the very least – loyalty to the England Rugby team. Joining in 'Take me down to the ball game…' indicates some enthusiasm for baseball.

But there are contexts in which joining in a song can be a dangerous thing. One of my favourite movies is the old black-and-white Second World War film *Casablanca*. Much of the story takes place in Rick's Café in wartime Casablanca. Through disappointment in love, the American café owner Rick has become cynical. But in a spine-tingling scene his true loyalty becomes apparent. A group of Nazi soldiers are rowdily singing an (anti-French) German patriotic anthem as they drink at their table. At this point the Czech resistance leader Victor Laszlo asks the band to strike up the Marseillaise. The band-leader looks anxiously at Rick who – in a defining moment of the drama – gives an affirmative nod; 'yes,' his nod indicates, 'you have my authority to play the Marseillaise'. Laszlo sings alone, and then others join in and the song drowns out the Nazi soldiers. As this defiant song of freedom fills the café each voice joining in identifies the singer with the struggle for freedom against the oppression of the Nazi regime. To join in that song at that time was a deeply significant thing to do. The Psalms are no less significant. For any Psalm I must ask: what will it mean for me to add my voice to this Psalm?

This is where it is vital to grasp the paradigm of the people of God assembled under the King. I will want to ask four questions:

1. **What did it mean for the original author of the Psalm to pray it?** We may know his name (most often David) or the group of singers to which he or she belonged (such as the Sons of Korah) or we may have no name. We may have some indication – from the superscription or the content – of the historical context that prompted the writing of the Psalm; or we may not. But we must ask this 'original author' question first.

2. Then we ask the closely related question of **what it meant for Old Covenant believers to pray this Psalm**. I often think of Simeon and Anna and their group of believers (of whom we read in Luke 2:25-38) gathering at the Temple to pray and wait for God to keep His Old Covenant promises. Although they appear at the start of the New Testament, they are Old Covenant believers. I would give Oscars to Simeon and Anna for Best Supporting Actor and Actress in the Bible drama! It is reasonable to suppose that they sang the Psalms in their prayer meetings. It is good to ask, what would it have meant to them to sing and pray this particular Psalm?

3. It is very natural to move from this question to ask: **what would it have meant for the believer Jesus of Nazareth to sing and pray this Psalm?** There will be

different answers for different Psalms, but always it is an important question and often opens up the New Covenant significance of a Psalm.

4. Finally, we ask **what it means for us as believers in Christ, having the Spirit of Christ, to sing and pray the Psalm 'in Christ'.** This is the answer we finally need before we decide whether or not to join in.

The Volitional Dimension: Make the Decision to join in

The final element is decision. Each individual man and woman in Rick's Café had a decision to make: will I, or will I not, sing the Marseillaise and identify myself with the Free French? When a Psalm is read to me, when I have understood the lyrics, when I have felt the emotions and affections of the tune, when I have thought carefully about the significance of the song, then it is decision time: Will I, or will I not, join my voice to the choir?

It is similar with Christian hymns. John Newton writes from his own experience, 'Amazing Grace – how sweet the sound that saved a wretch like me.' We may listen to a solo and think of the singer and how this was true for him or her. But when we join in, we affirm that Newton was not the only wretch needing grace to save him; we include ourselves. We read William Cowper's agonised questions: 'Where is the blessedness I knew, when first I saw the Lord? Where is the soul-refreshing view of Jesus and his word?' We feel the sadness of Cowper as he struggled with deep depression. But when we join in, we are doing something more; we admit that we too have times when we lose the felt wonder of Jesus; we too need to cry to God for gospel blessings in refreshment.

The Psalms are a little like that. The singer needs to decide to sing this song. The decision that is called for by a Psalm is the decision to enter into all that the Psalm expresses, to make the Psalm one's own. The Psalms open for us a window into a world of praise and prayer. They invite us not simply to look through the window, to observe and perhaps admire; we are called to enter through this window into this world, and to live in it. Or, to change the analogy, they call us not simply to listen with admiration to a solo performance, but to join the choir. There is all the difference in the world between studying a Psalm as a student and joining in singing it as a worshipper.

Augustine famously said that the human race could be divided into 'mockers and praisers,' those whose hearts are set to mock God and the things of God, and those who in the deepest level of their being have made the decision to praise God. Each Psalm forces this decision upon us: will we merely listen to others singing the Psalm or will we join in and make it our own?

The responses to the word of God that we find within the word of God are normative, authorised responses. We are invited, not only to listen and learn, but to join in.

> These…constitute normative responses in which the reader is invited to share and participate. We too must respond to injustice with laments and prayers for justice. We too must respond to God's mercy and love with sincere praise. We too must have imaginations captive to the vision of the kingdom of God. Not only our minds, but also our emotional responses are brought under scriptural authority.[7]

Brian Brock writes,

---

7. Kevin Vanhoozer, 'The Semantics of Biblical Literature,' in Carson and Woodbridge 1986:94.

'The metaphor of singing (more than reading or thinking) draws attention to the way an external word can
claim human action and affections and thus be inter-
nalized as a way of life.' Indeed – to use more technical
language – 'language worlds, if we enter them, can
orient and shape our lives.'[8]

In other words, if we join in the praying of the Psalms, we
will be changed deeply.

Guarding all four elements

Our task is didactic, affective, significant, and volitional.
We want to ask and answer four questions:

- Do I understand it? (the didactic question)

- Can I feel it? (the affective question)

- What will it mean to join in? (the significance
  question)

- Am I willing to join in? (the volitional
  question)

Some drive the instruction so hard, that the Psalm risks
travelling – like a bad university lecture – from the notes
of the preacher to the notebooks of the hearers without
engaging with the heart of either. Others skip the hard
work of instruction and go straight to the feelings; the
result is fluff, words sung with gusto, but the mind and
heart disengaged. Perhaps most often, we fail to press
home the volitional dimension, to exhort, challenge and
rouse our hearers to take the heart decision to make this
their own prayer.

---

8. Brock 2007:xvi.

Do not divorce music and meaning

Music is powerful for good and evil. Because it is so powerful, it has attendant dangers. One of the great dangers with Christian music is the unthinking divorce of music and meaning. A cynic once said that if you want to persuade someone to say something silly, put it in the lyrics of a song to a catchy tune. When music is decoupled from truth it can open a door for error and become an interloper into our souls. Augustine warns against letting the melodies distract from the words. Whenever he found 'the singing itself more moving than the truth which it conveys' he took this to be a 'grievous sin.'[9]

You need to pray a Psalm before you teach it

Only those who have authentically prayed a Psalm can, with integrity, teach others to pray it. A contemporary wrote of one preacher of the Psalms in the seventeenth century that he 'writes like one that knew the Singer's heart, and felt in his own the sanctifying power of what he wrote.' To know the singer's heart is to know the heart of Christ, whose Spirit breathed into the heart of the Psalmists.

There is no short cut to a focussed attentiveness of heart and mind; we must study, meditate on, and pray a Psalm before we are ready to teach others to pray. A sermon on a Psalm should never be, 'Now let me teach you how to pray it,' but rather, 'Let me show you how to join me in praying this Psalm together.'

The goal of preaching the Psalms
is that we pray the Psalms

Near the close of his life, God gives Moses a song to teach the people of Israel. In Deuteronomy 32 he teaches Israel

---

9. Augustine, *Confessions* Book X, Ch.33, quoted in Jaki 2001:5.

a song that sums up the message of the Law. Why a song? So that they will never forget. In generations to come, says the Lord, this song 'will not be forgotten' (Deut. 31:21). We remember songs long after we have forgotten spoken words. A snatch from an old tune comes back to us and we recall the words.

Gordon Wenham begins his book *The Psalter Reclaimed: Praying and Praising with the Psalms*, with this quotation from an eighteenth-century Scottish politician: 'Let me write the songs of a nation, and I care not who writes its laws.'[10] His point is well made. As Wenham writes elsewhere, 'the words hymn-writers and liturgists put on our lips in worship affect us profoundly: they teach us what to think and feel, the more effectively when they are put to music, so we can hum them to ourselves whenever we are inclined.'[11]

18. A Framework for preparing to teach a Psalm

Why a framework?

The purpose of this chapter is to build especially on the last chapter and to pull together some of the key lessons of this handbook into a method of preparation. You may find yourself bristling at being told how to prepare teaching on the Psalms, as if it can be done by a system, rather like painting by numbers. But think of it this way. I am a very poor cook (happily married to a very good cook). But from time to time I have a go at learning to cook. I need to be

---

10. Wenham 2013:13.

11. Gordon Wenham 'The Ethics of the Psalms' in Johnston and Firth 2005:177.

told how to prepare a dish from a really straightforward recipe book. I remember being stumped on one occasion, quite early on, when the recipe book said, 'First make the pancakes in the usual way.' I had no idea how to make pancakes, whether in a usual or an unusual way! I need to be told a simple method. My wife can look in the fridge, see what leftovers there are, and concoct something delicious; I cannot do that. Perhaps one day I will be able to, perhaps not. An experienced preacher of the Psalms can, and should, vary this method in all sorts of creative ways. But for many – perhaps most – of us, it will give a helpful start.

The big picture: Get up out of your seats!

Picture the people of God assembled on a concert hall platform, led by Jesus Christ their King as the lead singer and conductor, singing the praises and prayers of the Psalms. At the start of the teaching process both you and your hearers are sitting in the audience, listening to the performance. If we take the four stages outlined in the previous chapter (Cognitive, Affective, Impactual, and Volitional), the first three take place as we listen.

First, we attend carefully to the lyrics. What are the words the choir are singing as Jesus leads them? What do these words mean? Which voices do we hear? Who is speaking and to whom? Second, what is the (emotional, affectual) music that accompanies the words? What does this Psalm feel like?

And then, third, it begins to get personal, even awkward. As I sit in the audience, I have to ask myself: what will it mean for me to get out of my seat, walk up on the platform, and join the choir? With what desires, what prayers, what affections, what convictions, what commitments, will I be identifying myself? In his great evangelistic rallies, Billy Graham famously appealed to men and women to 'get up out of your seats' and come to the front to profess faith in Jesus Christ. Singing a Psalm is not unlike that. Just as it would be a big – and potentially embarrassing! – step to get out of my seat in a concert hall and join the choir, so it is a step of personal commitment to join from my heart in the praying of any Psalm[12]. The first three tasks of the Psalms teacher are to help our hearers listen attentively to the lyrics, feel sensitively the tune, and think carefully what it would mean to join in.

But then, finally, we need to press our hearers to take that decision. We need first to have taken that step ourselves; to exhort them to join in while I remain in my concert hall seat is like pushing my platoon out of the trenches, over the top, while staying safely behind myself. Only when I have begun to join in from the heart can I preach to others to join in. But join in they must, if the Psalm is to become theirs. It is this final step that is the hardest for a Psalms teacher; but without it we fail. If we and our hearers remain in our seats listening to the concert, then our preaching never moves beyond the role of a concert critic helping with the enjoyment of the entertainment. But our calling is to recruit for the choir!

Diagnostic questions
So let us take those four stages. Here are some diagnostic questions to help with preparation.

---

12. Wenham 2013:23-35 backs this up by considering Psalms as 'Speech Acts'. Wenham writes that 'Singing (the Psalms) commits us in attitudes, speech, and actions' (p. 25).

What do the Lyrics mean?

Context: are there indications of the context of the Psalm,

- from a superscription?

- from the content of the Psalm? (e.g. events in Israel's history that might have prompted it)

- from its placing in the Psalter?

Structure: what structural markers are there (if any)? (Don't try to superimpose a structure that isn't there; not all Psalms have clear structural markers and there is no *a priori* reason why they should.)

- are there clear breaks or changes of theme, tone, or subject matter?

- is there a progression as we move through the Psalm?

- is there an inclusion ('bookends') that repeat a motif at the start and end of the Psalm?

Repetitions: remember that synonyms or antonyms may be used to reiterate a theme

- are there repeated words or phrases (or the use of synonyms to repeat ideas)?

- is there a refrain?

Translation issues:

- are there significant differences between reliable English translations?

- are there footnotes to indicate manuscript uncertainty?

- in particular, do different translations translate any of the tenses differently?

Imagery: what images are used in the wording of the Psalm?

Allusions: are there quotations or (more often) allusions to other parts of the Old Testament or echoes in the New Testament? In particular, refer to chapters 9-14 to help pick up allusions to Creation, Abraham, Exodus, Sinai, Zion, or Exile.

Voices and Audiences: who is speaking, and to whom, in the different parts of the Psalm? (see chapter 8)

What does the Tune feel like?
Read the Psalm aloud.

- What musical instruments would you choose to accompany it, or the different parts of it?

- Would you sing it – or the different parts of it – in a major or a minor key?

- What feelings, longings, hopes, or fears does the Psalm express and encourage us to echo as we join in?

Look carefully at the way the parallelism works.

- does the second line intensify the first line?

- …or contrast with it so that we feel both positive and negative?

Revisit the imagery. What affections (or aversions) do these images express?

What about the allusions to elsewhere in the Old Testament? What memories would these conjure up in biblically-literate Old Covenant believers? How would it make them feel? What longings or fears would be stirred up by these allusions?

What would it mean to join in?
Before answering the question of what it will mean if I decide to join in, ask first,

- what commitments, convictions, affections and aversions were expressed by the original author?

- …and by Old Covenant believers singing the Psalm from the heart with faith?

- …and finally by Jesus Christ as the fulfilment of Old Covenant faith?

At some stage, we need to do the Old Covenant to New Covenant translation, taking – for example – the theme of the temple and seeing how the New Testament understands its fulfilment in Jesus and the church of Jesus.

But then ask – and express as clearly as you can – what will it mean for us as New Covenant believers, 'in Christ' to join the choir and sing this Psalm?

Will I, or will I not, join in?
As a Psalms teacher, think yourself into the shoes of those whom you teach, and ask yourself,

- what obstacles in the hearts of my hearers (and my own heart) will make us reluctant to join the choir?

- what incentives does the Psalm offer to encourage us to join in?

- have I honestly joined in myself?

- how best can I exhort my hearers to get out of their audience seats and join the choir?

Constructing the skeleton of a sermon or talk to teach this Psalm

Remember, the aim of the teaching is that both we and our hearers will get out of our seats and pray the Psalm with understanding, feeling, and conviction. This will only happen in answer to prayer as God sovereignly works in your heart and the hearts of your hearers. Under God, there are many ways of teaching that will be geared to achieve this. Here is one strategy you may like to try.

1. Follow the structure of the Psalm. Take its main divisions, if it has a clear sequential structure. Or take its main interwoven themes, if they appear alongside one another rather than sequentially. Express each of these divisions or themes as a clear teaching (or praying) point.

2. Decide what is the dominant thrust of the Psalm in terms of the convictions it expresses or the desires it encapsulates. Think about the obstacles to this and begin with a 'hook' that asks a question that leads into the heart of the Psalm and persuades your hearers that it will be worth their while to listen.

3. Conclude by pressing home the main thrust of application, the main commitment expressed by joining in, and exhorting your hearers to take that decision of the will to join in.

4. At the end, perhaps invite your hearers to join you in saying the Psalm aloud together as a prayer.

19. Planning a Teaching Series on the Psalms

How do you set about planning a teaching series – perhaps sermons, youth group talks, or studies for Bible study groups? While there is nothing wrong with starting with Psalm 1 and gradually working through to Psalm 150, there will be better ways to introduce the Psalter to those unfamiliar with praying the Psalms.

Here are some ideas.

Introductory series

Here are five ideas for introductory series.

'Lord, teach us to pray' (learning to
pray the Psalms with Jesus)

The aim of this series is to introduce the paradigm of praying the Psalms in Christ.

1.	Praying under pressure with Jesus	Psalm 3
2.	Enjoying the righteousness of Jesus	Psalm 16
3.	Knowing the sufferings of Jesus	Psalm 88
4.	Waiting for rescue with Jesus	Psalm 126
5.	Yearning for judgment with Jesus	Psalm 109
6.	Learning to praise with Jesus	Psalm 146

Of these, number 5 is the hardest. You may want to omit this, depending on the maturity of your hearers.

Pathways into the Psalms

Another idea is to give a basic orientation to the Psalter as a whole. For example, this series takes some of the key Psalms at the start and end and at one of the important 'joins' between two books.

1. The Front Door
   (1) Who does best in the end?   Psalm 1

2. The Front Door
   (2) Who rules the world in the end?   Psalm 2

3. End of part 2
   What kind of ruler will rule the world   Psalm 72

4. Start of part 3
   But why does it all go wrong in
   the middle?   Psalm 73

5. The Climax
   How can we praise when it's so bad?   Psalm 150

Jesus in the Psalms
If people find it hard to connect the Psalms with Jesus, you could teach a series on some of the Psalms explicitly quoted by, or of, Jesus in the New Testament. In each case, the aim is to show how the New Testament gives us a pointer that the whole of the Psalm is either about the Messiah or finds its fulfilment on the lips of the Messiah.

1. The Royal Son
   Psalm 2 (You are my Son) – with e.g. Mark 1:11

2. The Ruling Man
   Psalm 8 (ruler over the work of your hands) – with
   Hebrews 2:5-9

3. The Resurrected Man
   Psalm 16 (nor will you let your faithful one see decay)
   – with Acts 2:25-32

4. The Godforsaken Innocent
   Psalm 22 (My God, my God, why have you forsaken
   me?) – with Mark 15:34

5. The True Believer
   Psalm 31 (Into your hands I commit my spirit) – with
   Luke 23:46

6. The Perfect Sacrifice
   Psalm 40 (…in the scroll of the book it is written of
   me) – with Heb.10:5-10

7. The Comfortless Sufferer
   Psalm 69 (they gave me vinegar for my thirst) – with
   allusions all four gospels

8. The greater than David
   Psalm 110 (The LORD says to my Lord…) – with
   Matthew 22:41-46

Theme Music in the Psalms
You could take one Psalm from each of the common themes
as a way in, for example:

1. Singing Creation in the Psalms   Psalm 104
2. Rejoicing in Abraham in the Psalms   Psalm 105
3. Celebrating Redemption in the Psalms   Exodus 15
4. Remembering Sinai in the Psalms   Psalm 37
5. Playing the music of Zion in the Psalms   Psalm 87
6. Grieving the Exile in the Psalms   Psalm 74

Voices in the Psalms
A series introducing the concept of Jesus leading His people
and what it means to have 'praising conversations'

1. Backing the solo of Jesus
   Psalm 3 (an individual Psalm of the King)

2. Joining the choir of Jesus
   Psalm 68 (a corporate Psalm led by the King)

3. Singing the beauty of Jesus
   Psalm 45

4. Hearing the honour of Jesus
   Psalm 110 (hearing the Father praise Jesus)

5. Heeding the voice of Jesus
   Psalm 37 (a Psalm of instruction)

6. Praying for the victory of Jesus
   Psalm 20

7. Praising God with Jesus
   Psalm 145

Collections within the Psalter

If you decide to include some Psalms teaching as a regular ingredient to your year-by-year teaching programme, you could use the collections signalled within the Psalter itself and tackle one each year. For the longer collections, you might choose to use just a selection.

Korah Psalms (mostly 42/3-49)

1. Psalm 42/3 Misery away from Christ

2. Psalm 44   Suffering with Christ

3. Psalm 45   Christ the beautiful Bridegroom

4. Psalm 46   Christ the Victor

5. Psalm 47   Loyalty to Christ

6. Psalm 48   Safety in Christ

7. Psalm 49   Facing death with Christ

Asaph Psalms (mostly 73-83)

1. Psalm 73   Why do the wicked prosper?

2. Psalm 74   How long, O Lord?

3. Psalm 75   Will God ever punish evil?

4. Psalm 76   Can evil praise God?

5. Psalm 77   Has God forgotten to be gracious?

6. Psalm 78   Lessons from history

7. Psalm 79   Praising the angry God

8. Psalm 80   Restore, O God

9. Psalm 81   I wish you would listen!

10. Psalm 82   God and the gods

11. Psalm 83   A plea for justice

Songs of Ascents (120-134)

1. Psalm 120   The misery of strife outside Christ

2. Psalm 121   The watchful God in Christ

3. Psalm 122   The joy of being in Christ

4. Psalm 123   The cry for mercy in Christ

5. Psalm 124   The narrow escape through Christ

6. Psalm 125   The peace of Christ

7. Psalm 126   Restore our fortunes in Christ

8. Psalm 127   The builder of Christ's house

9. Psalm 128   The prosperity of Christ's family

10. Psalm 129   The danger of hating Christ's people

11. Psalm 130   Hoping in Christ

12. Psalm 131   The calmed heart in Christ

13. Psalm 132   Christ the king

14. Psalm 133   All one in Christ

15. Psalm 134   Blessing in Christ

The Hallelujah Chorus (146-150)

1. Psalm 146   Praise the God of the gospel
2. Psalm 147   Praise the God of the church
3. Psalm 148   Praise the God of creation
4. Psalm 149   Praise the God of judgment
5. Psalm 150   Praise the God of the Bible

A series going through one long Psalm

Another idea is to work through one longer Psalm (such as 18, 78, 89, 106, or 119) in smaller sections. *Bible Delight* works right through Psalm 119.[13] For a shorter series, here is an example from Psalm 89.

1. Psalm 89:1-18   The faithfulness of God

2. Psalm 89:19-37   The certainty of the King

3. Psalm 89:38-52   How long, O Lord?

A Psalm every Sunday

One church I know has, for several years now, included one Psalm in their Sunday meeting, not as the main preaching series, but as a part of their corporate prayer and praise together. They have begun with Psalm 1, continued with Psalm 2 the following week, and so on until they reach Psalm 150, when they start again. (I imagine they divide up Psalm 119!)

To educate the congregation about praying the Psalms, they

- read the Psalm together aloud

- have a very short teaching slot to give pointers to praying it

- sing a metrical version of the Psalm

13. Ash 2008.

The cumulative effect of this over the years is a congregation for whom praying the Psalms (all the Psalms) has become a normal part of the way they relate to God. In so doing they have reintegrated themselves into a significant part of Christian history.

What will Volume Two include?

Volume Two begins with a structural overview of the Psalter as a whole. This will help us see the significance of the *literary* context of a Psalm, where it fits into the flow of the Psalms as a whole.

After that there is a brief entry for each of the 150 Psalms in which I try to provide two things that the commentaries very rarely offer. First, to 'line up' the Psalm for a persuasive Christian reading, so that we see how this particular Psalm – with all its individuality – finds its fulfilment in Christ. In order to do this, I also make a brief comment on what voice or voices we hear in different parts of the Psalm (referring back to chapter 5).

The second aim is to indicate the main lines of appropriate and valid response to which this Psalm calls us; what will it mean for us to 'get up out of our seats' and take our place in Christ's choir to join in the singing of this Psalm?

Conclusion:

HOW THE PSALMS RESHAPE OUR PRAYERS

I want to reflect, at the end of this handbook, about some of the main ways in which praying the Psalms will change the way we pray. The Psalms are not the only way in which God will shape our prayers and praises, but they are one of the main ways.

Augustine wrote, 'Attune your heart to the Psalms. If the Psalm prays, you pray; if it mourns, you mourn; if it hopes, you hope; if it fears, you fear. Everything in the Psalter is the mirror of the soul.'[1]

Here are four ways we will pray differently after learning to pray the Psalms.

Our prayers will, more explicitly, be centred on Christ
We know that 'every spiritual blessing' (that is, every blessing given by the Holy Spirit, which is every true blessing) comes to us 'in Christ' (Eph. 1:3). No blessing

---

1. quoted by Herbert Lockyer, 'In Wonder of the Psalms,' *Christianity Today* 28.4 (March 2nd, 1984), p. 76. I am grateful to John F. Evans for this quotation.

comes to us outside of Christ. Learning to pray the Psalms in Christ will help us never to take Christ for granted, but to understand and feel more deeply the full variety of blessing that comes to us in Him. The Psalms will – as Augustine put it – settle us more deeply in Christ.

Our prayers will be more corporate and less individualistic

When we learn to pray the Psalms as the people of Christ, corporately with Christ our song-leader, even our individual prayers will be tied in to the bigger prayers of the whole Church of God. This will lift our eyes beyond the narrow horizons of our individual concerns.

We will have a broader and richer spectrum from lament to praise

We default to being rather monochrome in the emotions and affections represented by our prayers. The Psalms will train us to express, along with the Church of Christ, a wide and deep range of experience and emotion, from the depths to the heights.

We will learn to be more deeply concerned for the honour of God in the holiness of Christ's Church

The Spirit of God breathes into the hearts of the Psalmists the passion of Jesus Christ for the honour of God. Such passion will gradually get under our skin and change our passions from within, so that we care less about our own reputation, comfort, or success, and a great deal more for the honour of God expressed in the building and integrity of Christ's Church. This will flow out in our prayers.

Bibliography

Commentaries on the Psalms

Allen, L. C. (2002), *Psalms 101-150* [Waco, Texas: Word Biblical Commentary]

Augustine (2004), *Expositions on the Psalms* [Peabody, Mass.: Hendrickson, Nicene and Post-Nicene Fathers vol. 10, 4th printing]

Calvin (1993), *Commentaries on the Psalms*, Vols. 4, 5, 6 of Calvin's Commentaries [Grand Rapids, Michigan: Baker]

Craigie, P. C. (1983), *Psalms 1-50* [Waco, Texas: Word Biblical Commentary]

Goldingay, J. (2006-8), *Psalms* [Grand Rapids, Michigan: Baker Academic, 3 vols]

Grogan, G. W. (2008), *Psalms* [Grand Rapids, Michigan: Eerdmans, The Two Horizons Old Testament Commentary]

Harman, A. (2011), *Psalms* [Ross-Shire: Christian Focus Mentor Commentary, 2 vols]

Jaki, S. (2001), *Praying the Psalms: A Commentary* [Grand Rapids, Michigan: Eerdmans]

Kidner, D. (1973-5), *Psalms* [London: IVP, 2 vols.]

Kirkpatrick, A. F. (1892-1903), *The Book of Psalms* [Cambridge University Press, 3 vols]

Kraus, H. J. (1993), *Psalms* [ET Minneapolis: Fortress Press, 2 vols]

Lane, E. (1993), *Psalms* [Ross-Shire: Christian Focus, 2 vols]

Longman, T. (2004), *Psalms* [Nottingham: IVP]

Mays, J. L. (1994), *Psalms* [Louisville: John Knox Press, Interpretation Series]

Perowne, J. J. S. (1898), *The Book of Psalms* [Andover, Mass.: Warren F. Draper]

Schaefer, K. (2001), *Psalms* [Collegeville, Minnesota: The Liturgical Press]

Spurgeon, C. (1993), *Psalms* [Wheaton, Illinois: Crossway Classic Commentaries, 2 vols]

Tate, M. E. (1990), *Psalms 51-100* [Waco, Texas: Word Biblical Commentary]

VanGemeren, W. A. (2008), *Psalms* [Grand Rapids, Michigan: Zondervan, The Expositor's Bible Commentary, vol.5]

Wilcock, M. (2001), *Psalms* 2 vols [Nottingham: IVP Bible Speaks Today]

Wilson, G. H. (2002), *Psalms*, [Grand Rapids: Zondervan NIVAC series]

Other Sources

Adams, J. E. (1991), *War Psalms of the Prince of Peace: Lessons from the Imprecatory Psalms* [Phillipsburg, New Jersey: P&R]

Anderson, B. W. (1970), *Out of the Depths: The Psalms speak for us today* [Philadelphia: Westminster Press]

Ash, C. B. G. (2003), *Marriage: Sex in the Service of God* [Nottingham: IVP]

Ash, C. B. G. (2009), *Teaching Romans* 2 vols [Ross-Shire: Christian Focus]

Ash, C. B. G. (2008), *Bible Delight: Psalm 119 for the Bible teacher and Bible hearer* [Ross-Shire: Christian Focus]

Ash, C. B. G. (2010), *Remaking a Broken World* [Milton Keynes: Authentic Media]

Ash, C. B. G. (2014), *Job: the wisdom of the Cross* [Wheaton, Illinois: Crossway Preaching the Word series]

Barth, C. F. (1966), *Introduction to the Psalms* [Oxford: Basil Blackwell]

Bockmuehl, M. (1997), *The Epistle to the Philippians* [London: A&C Black]

Bonhoeffer, D. (1960), *Prisoner for God: Letters and Papers from Prison* [New York: Macmillan]

Bonhoeffer, D. (2005), *Life Together* and *Prayerbook of the Bible* [Minneapolis: Fortress Press, Dietrich Bonhoeffer Works Vol.5, paperback edition]

Brock, B. (2007), *Singing the Ethos of God: On the Place of Christian Ethics in Scripture* [Grand Rapids, Michigan: Eerdmans]

Brueggemann, W. (1984), *The Message of the Psalms* [Augsburg, Minneapolis: Fortress]

Brueggemann, W. (2007), *Praying the Psalms* [Eugene, Oregon: Cascade Books]

Brueggemann, W. (2010), *Israel's Praise: Doxology against Idolatry and Ideology* [Philadelphia: Eerdmans]

Bullock, C. H. (2001), *Encountering the Book of Psalms* [Grand Rapids, Michigan: Baker Academic]

Burnside, J. (2011), *God, Justice, and Society* [Oxford: University Press]

Carson, D. A. and Woodbridge, P.D. (1986), *Hermeneutics, Authority and Canon* [Grand Rapids, Michigan: Zondervan]

Calvin, *Preface to Commentary on the Psalms* Vol. 4 of Calvin's Commentaries [Grand Rapids, Michigan: Baker, 1993]

Chester, T. (2005), *Delighting in the Trinity* [Oxford: Monarch]

Davis, D. R. (2010), *The Way of the Righteous in the Muck of Life: Psalms 1-12* [Ross-Shire: Christian Focus]

De Vaux, R. (1973), *Ancient Israel: Its Life and Institutions* ET [London: Darton, Longman and Todd]

Goldsworthy, G. (2003), *Prayer and the Knowledge of God* [Leicester: IVP]

Grogan, G. (2001), *Prayer, Praise and Prophecy: A Theology of the Psalms* [Ross-Shire: Christian Focus]

Holladay, W. L. (1996), *The Psalms through Three Thousand Years: Prayerbook of a Cloud of Witnesses* [Minneapolis: Fortress Press]

Johnston, P. S. & Firth, D. G. (eds.)(2005), *Interpreting the Psalms: Issues and Approaches* [Leicester: IVP Apollos]

Keller, T. (2015), *My Rock, My Refuge: A Year of Daily Devotions in the Psalms* [London: Hodder]

Kidd, R. M. (2005), *With One Voice: Discovering Christ's Song in Our Worship* [Grand Rapids, Michigan: Baker]

Kidner, D. (1972), *Hard Sayings* [London: IVP]

Knox, R. A. (1950), *Enthusiasm* [Oxford: University Press]

Kraus, H. J. (1992), *Theology of the Psalms* [Minneapolis: Fortress Press]

Lefebvre, M. (2010), *Singing the Songs of Jesus: Revisiting the Psalms* [Ross-Shire: Christian Focus]

Lewis, C. S. (1961), *Reflections on the Psalms* [London: Harper Collins]

Longman, T. (1988), *How to Read the Psalms* [Downers Grove, Illinois: IVP]

Luther (1960), *Preface to the Psalter*, in *Luther's Works*, vol.35 [Philadelphia: Fortress Press]

McCann, J. C. (Ed)(1993a), *Shape and Shaping of the Psalter* [Sheffield: JSOT Supplement Series 159]

McCann, J. C. (1993b), *A Theological Introduction to the Book of Psalms: The Psalms as Torah* [Nashville: Abingdon Press]

McLarney, G. M. (2014), *St Augustine's Interpretation of the Psalms of Ascent* [Washington, D.C.: The Catholic University of America Press]

Millar, J. G. (2016), *Calling on the Name of the Lord: A biblical theology of prayer* [Downers Grove, Illinois: Apollos New Studies in Biblical Theology]

Miller, P. D. (1986), *Interpreting the Psalms* [Philadelphia: Fortress Press]

Mitchell, D. C. (1997), *Message of the Psalter: An Eschatological Programme in the Book of Psalms* JSOTSup 252 [Sheffield: JSOT Press]

O'Brien, P. (1999), *The Letter to the Ephesians* [Leicester: Apollos Pillar NT Commentary]

O'Donovan, O. (1994), *Resurrection and Moral Order: An Outline for Evangelical Ethics* [Leicester: IVP]

Roberts, A. (2009), *Masters and Commanders* [London: Penguin]

Peterson, E. H. (1991), *Answering God: The Psalms as Tools for Prayer* [New York: Harper Collins, paperback]

Ryken, P. G. (2010), *Ecclesiastes* [Wheaton, Illinois: Crossway]

Sanders, F. (2010), *The Deep Things of God* [Wheaton, Illinois: Crossway]

Shead, A. G. (ed.)(2013), *Stirred by a Noble Theme: The book of Psalms in the life of the church* [Leicester: IVP Apollos]

Waltke, B. K. and Houston, J.M. (1988), *The Psalms as Christian Worship* [Grand Rapids, Michigan: Fortress Press]

Waltke, B. K. (1981), 'A Canonical Process Approach to the Psalms' in *Tradition and Testament*, ed. John S.Feinberg and Paul D. Feinberg [Chicago: Moody Press, 1981]

Westermann, C. (1965), *The Praise of God in the Psalms* [ET Richmond, Virginia: John Knox Press]

Westermann, C. (1981), *Praise and Lament in the Psalms* [ET Atlanta: John Knox Press]

Wilson, G. H. (1985), *The Editing of the Hebrew Psalter* [Chico, California: Scholars Press SBL Dissertation Series]

Wenham, G. (2012), *Psalms as Torah: Reading Biblical Song Ethically* [Grand Rapids, Michigan: Baker]

Wenham, G. (2013), *The Psalter Reclaimed: Praying and Praising with the Psalms* [Wheaton, Illinois: Crossway]

PT RESOURCES

RESOURCES FOR PREACHERS AND
BIBLE TEACHERS

PT Resources, a ministry of The Proclamation Trust, provides a range of multimedia resources for preachers and Bible teachers.

Teach the Bible Series (Christian Focus & PT Resources)
The Teaching the Bible Series, published jointly with Christian Focus Publications, is written by preachers, for preachers, and is specifically geared to the purpose of God's Word – its proclamation as living truth. Books in the series aim to help the reader move beyond simply understanding a text to communicating and applying it.

Current titles include: *Teaching Numbers, Teaching 1 Kings, Teaching Isaiah, Teaching Daniel, Teaching Psalms (Volume 1), Teaching Amos, Teaching Matthew, Teaching Acts, Teaching Romans (in two volumes), Teaching Ephesians, Teaching 1 and 2 Thessalonians, Teaching 1 Timothy, Teaching 2 Timothy, Teaching 1 Peter, Teaching 1, 2, 3 John,* and *Teaching the Christian Hope.*

Practical Preacher series

PT Resources publish a number of books addressing practical issues for preachers. These include *The Priority of Preaching, Bible Delight, Hearing the Spirit* and *The Ministry Medical*.

Online resources

We publish a large number of audio resources online, all of which are free to download. These are searchable through our website by speaker, date, topic and Bible book. The resources include:

+ sermon series; examples of great preaching which not only demonstrate faithful principles but which will refresh and encourage the heart of the preacher

+ instructions; audio which helps the teacher or preacher understand, open up and teach individual books of the Bible by getting to grips with their central message and purpose

+ conference recordings; audio from all our conferences including the annual Evangelical Ministry Assembly. These talks discuss ministry and preaching issues.

An increasing number of resources are also available in video download form.

Online DVD

PT Resources have recently published online our collection of instructional videos by David Jackman. This material has been taught over the past 20 years on our PT Cornhill training course and around the world. It gives step by step instructions on handling each genre of biblical literature. There is also an online workbook. The videos are suitable for preachers and those teaching the Bible in a variety of different contexts. Access to all the videos is free of charge.

The Proclaimer

Visit the Proclaimer blog for regular updates on matters to do with preaching. This is a short, punchy blog refreshed daily which is written by preachers and for preachers. It can be accessed via the PT website or through www.theproclaimer.org.uk.

TEACHING
DANIEL

From text to message

ROBERT FYALL & ROBIN SYDSERFF

SERIES EDITORS: DAVID JACKMAN & ADRIAN REYNOLDS

Teaching Daniel
by Robert Fyall & Robin Sydserff

This useful resource, alongside the others in this growing 'Teaching the Bible Series', is for those who have the privilege and joy of teaching or preaching a particular book or theme from the Bible. Whether you're a leader of a small group, preacher or a youth worker, it will help you to communicate the message of Daniel.

Bob Fyall is Senior Tutor in Ministry for the Cornhill Training Course (Scotland). Prior to that he was the Director of Rutherford House, Edinburgh. He is an experienced pastor, preacher and Old Testament scholar.

Robin Sydserff is the minister of Chalmers Church, Edinburgh, having previously served as Director of Ministry for Cornhill.

ISBN: 978-1-84550-457-1

TEACHING
NUMBERS
From text to message
ADRIAN REYNOLDS

SERIES EDITORS: DAVID JACKMAN & ADRIAN REYNOLDS

TEACHING
1 KINGS
From text to message
BOB FYALL

SERIES EDITORS: DAVID JACKMAN & ADRIAN REYNOLDS

TEACHING
AMOS
From text to message
BOB FYALL

SERIES EDITORS: DAVID JACKMAN & ROBIN SYDSERFF

TEACHING
ACTS
Unlocking the book of Acts
for the Bible Teacher
DAVID COOK

SERIES EDITORS: DAVID JACKMAN & ROBIN SYDSERFF

TEACHING
EPHESIANS
From text to message
SIMON AUSTEN

SERIES EDITORS: DAVID JACKMAN & ADRIAN REYNOLDS

TEACHING
1 & 2 THESSALONIANS
From text to message
ANGUS MACLEAY

SERIES EDITORS: DAVID JACKMAN & ADRIAN REYNOLDS

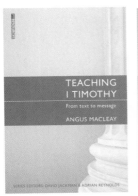

TEACHING
1 TIMOTHY
From text to message
ANGUS MACLEAY

SERIES EDITORS: DAVID JACKMAN & ADRIAN REYNOLDS

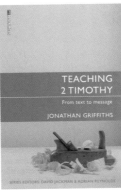

TEACHING
2 TIMOTHY
From text to message
JONATHAN GRIFFITHS

SERIES EDITORS: DAVID JACKMAN & ADRIAN REYNOLDS

TEACHING
1 PETER
Unlocking the book of 1 Peter
for the Bible Teacher
ANGUS MACLEAY

SERIES EDITORS: DAVID JACKMAN & ROBIN SYDSERFF

Teaching Numbers
Adrian Reynolds
ISBN 978-1-78191-156-3

Teaching 1 Kings
Robert Fyall
ISBN 978-1-78191-605-6

Teaching Isaiah
David Jackman
ISBN 978-1-84550-565-3

Teaching Amos
Robert Fyall
ISBN 978-1-84550-142-6

Teaching Matthew
William Philip & David Jackman
ISBN 978-1-84550-480-9

Teaching Acts
David Cook
ISBN 978-1-84550-255-3

Teaching Romans (volume 1 & 2)
Christopher Ash
ISBN 978-1-84550-455-7 (1) & ISBN 978-1-84550-456-4 (2)

Teaching Ephesians
Simon Austen
ISBN 978-1-84550-684-1

Teaching 1 & 2 Thessalonians
Angus MacLeay
ISBN 978-1-78191-325-3

Teaching 1 Timothy
Angus MacLeay
ISBN 978-1-84550-808-1

Teaching 2 Timothy
Jonathan Griffiths
ISBN 978-1-78191-389-5

Teaching 1 Peter
Angus MacLeay
ISBN 978-1-84550-347-5

Teaching 1, 2, 3 John
Mervyn Eloff
ISBN 978-1-78191-832-6

Teaching the Christian Hope
David Jackman
ISBN 978-1-85792-518-0

Christian Focus Publications

Our mission statement –

STAYING FAITHFUL

In dependence upon God we seek to impact the world through literature faithful to His infallible Word, the Bible. Our aim is to ensure that the Lord Jesus Christ is presented as the only hope to obtain forgiveness of sin, live a useful life and look forward to heaven with Him.

Our books are published in four imprints:

CHRISTIAN
FOCUS

Popular works including biographies, commentaries, basic doc-trine and Christian living.

CHRISTIAN
HERITAGE

Books representing some of the best material from the rich heritage of the church.

MENTOR

Books written at a level suitable for Bible College and seminary students, pastors, and other serious readers. The imprint includes commentaries, doctrinal studies, examination of current issues and church history.

CF4•K

Children's books for quality Bible teaching and for all age groups: Sunday school curriculum, puzzle and activity books; personal and family devotional titles, biographies and inspirational stories – because you are never too young to know Jesus!

Christian Focus Publications Ltd,
Geanies House, Fearn, Ross-shire,
IV20 1TW, Scotland, United Kingdom.
www.christianfocus.com